AMERICA THROUGH A TRAIN WINDOW

A travelogue

LIZ BAINS

ABOUT THE AUTHOR

Liz Bains is an undiscovered stand-up comic and long-term resident of Dubai. For 10 years, she was the editor of the Middle East's leading business magazine, before realising job security was not for her and she was better suited to the life of a frustrated, impoverished creative. Through buying this book, you are helping free a woman from corporate slavery. Even if you never finish reading it, you have done a great thing, so pat yourself on the back.

This travelogue is based on jottings made in notebooks, on beer mats and random scraps of paper between November and December 2015.

First printing: 2020.

'The free, exploring mind of the individual human is the most valuable thing in the world.'

John Steinbeck, *East of Eden*

This book is dedicated to the memory of
my mum and dad.
Every day, I still strive to make you proud of me.

ACKNOWLEDGEMENTS

I would like to thank the following people for their support during the preparation of this book: Angela, who made me promise to write a blog while travelling around America - you were taken from us too soon; Costa, who read my blog and emailed me to say I had to do something more with it - you gave me the courage to attempt this book; Louise, who has listened patiently to my every frustration and medical complaint for years - our weekly meet-ups help to keep me sane, so I forgive you for telling me to burn my manuscript, when it looked like this book would never be finished; Marianne, who read a terrible early draft and motivated me to continue; Mina, who, in addition to being my comedy mentor, provided me with a role model for my new life of sobriety - I'm grateful to you for always pushing my boundaries and hopefully, one day, I will no longer have to pay you to be my friend; Amr, who stepped in at the last minute after my original designer let me down and produced this fantastic cover and map; and lastly, my brother and sister for giving their seal of approval to the final draft - it is, after all, your opinion alone that matters as you have spent a lifetime telling me.

CONTENTS

Boston
Washington
New York
Miami
Key West
90 miles TO CUBA
Nashville
Chicago
New Orleans
Mississippi River
San Antonio
Yuma
San Francisco
HOLLYWOOD
Los Angeles

This map is highly inaccurate and should not be used when out trekking.

Created by Ann Blaxel

GONE FISHING

IT WAS AN EASY sell to the bosses. 'Can I have a sabbatical, please? I am turning 40.' The very use of the word 40 hinted at a mid-life crisis, so I knew they weren't going to refuse me yet another career break. For good measure though, and to appeal to their own insecurities, I threw in the additional words 'childless spinster' and with that the deal was done: a month's unpaid leave for every decade I had spent on the planet.

Forty is just a number, one greater than 39 and one less than 41, yet society has attached such significance to this birthday and other similarly rounded ages that it has become something we are meant to dread. It didn't bother me. I welcomed its arrival as providing the perfect excuse to go off adventuring around the world again, because travelling is what I do best.

Travelling makes me feel alive. It educates me. It challenges me. It reminds me what a beautiful world we live in and how blessed I am in my life. Nothing beats the thrill of arriving in a new city or country, with all the exploring that lies ahead. Best of all are those places where culture shock hits, creating an exhilarating mix of excitement and trepidation.

The first time I went abroad was when my maternal uncle took me on a jaunt through France, Germany, Switzerland and possibly

Austria. It involved missing school for a fortnight, which in itself was a joy as I briefly became one of the cool kids, albeit one who wore knee-length, white 'virgin' socks.

The holiday didn't fill me with an immediate love for travelling. I must have been about 11 or 12 and I still suffered with motion sickness, which had plagued me since my pram days and always added an element of drama to the family venturing beyond the bottom of our driveway. The winding Alpine passes inevitably got to poor little me lolling around on the back seat. A timid creature, taught to speak only when spoken to, I couldn't bring myself to pipe up and say I was feeling sick. I fought the nausea to no avail and ended up showering the back of the hire car with that morning's *pain au chocolat* and vestiges of the previous night's dinner.

Thirty minutes later, feeling peckish, I wolfed a load of monkey nuts washed down with Pepsi, only to spray the contents of my stomach around the car again in a design that would have made Jackson Pollock proud. An original *Shimmering Substance*. The scent would linger for the rest of the holiday.

A tame exploration of Baden-Baden and the Black Forest left me with little enthusiasm for Germany and the dirty look I got from the hotel cleaners in Basel, when they caught me climbing through a window onto the balcony rather than using the door, imbued me with a profound dislike of the clearly boring Swiss. The culmination of the trip was a stay at a *gîte* in the leafy Dordogne region of France, my abiding memory of which was being an awful, verging on cruel, babysitter for my cousins.

Witnessing the majestic Mont Blanc with its glaciers did, however, provide a sense of wonderment at the world outside my home village of Ditton in the UK, famed for nothing but a passing mention in the Domesday Book. And seeing my uncle plot our route across the car bonnet each morning led to my life-long fascination for maps. On reflection, I can see the trip also left me with the impression that travel should foremostly be character-building, rather than relaxing, and that pleasure is derived from overcoming the odds to reach a destination.

That is why I usually opt for the most challenging means of getting from A to B and why, to kick off my 40th birthday celebrations, I have pencilled a vague plan to travel around America by train, taking in the famous sights of New York, Washington, Chicago, San Francisco, Los Angeles, Las Vegas, New Orleans and Nashville.

Anyone who knew me during my university years in the mid-1990s would be surprised at this choice of destination as I was fervently anti-American back then. I shunned all the popular clothing brands, avoided blockbuster films and cult television series (I have never seen an episode of *Friends*), and I refused any kind of fast food, no matter how drunk or hungry I was. I simply didn't want to be seen supporting Washington, the world's self-appointed policeman. As far as I was concerned, chewing gum was the work of the devil.

My anti-Americanism was not rooted in a moralistic abhorrence of the White House interfering in the politics of other countries, rather, it stemmed from a sense of wounded colonial pride - quite controversial in 2020, I know. Following the collapse of the Soviet Union, the US was constantly being referred to as the world's only superpower and Chris Patten's tears as he handed Hong Kong over to the Chinese Communist Party on that rainy night in 1997 only served to reinforce how far us British had fallen. It was a new age of globalisation and this time America was in charge. When Bush-Clinton-Bush said jump, our representatives in Downing Street got their trampolines out and asked how high. With the well-founded reasoning of a teenage temper tantrum, I swore I would never set foot in the country.

I'd had some real life encounters with Americans too, mostly while interrailing around Europe in 1994, and their endless high spirits exhausted me. I learnt to spot them a mile off because of their Tigger-like boisterousness. I found them abrasive and their confidence overbearing; they always seemed to be in a hurry to shove an opinion down my throat.

Several years later, an incident which I have never been able to forget further clouded my opinion of Americans. I was on a tour bus going from Warsaw to Auschwitz and an American woman tried to board without a ticket. She said she would pay when we arrived as she needed a cashpoint. Bank machines were hard to come by in any Polish city at the turn of the century, and there certainly weren't any in former concentration camps. The woman refused to leave the bus and became aggressive with the tour guide, screaming and shouting, and throwing all sorts of insults at her. Her behaviour would have been disgusting no matter where were going, but the fact that our destination was Auschwitz made it all the more shameful. Only when the rest of us put our money together to buy her a ticket, did the woman begin to calm down. I glowered at her for the entire bus journey, intermittently tutting 'Americans'.

Two things have since served to soften my stance and make me wish to understand the US better. A decade living in Dubai has left me curious to see the cities on which it has modelled itself. Before that though, it was the horrific terrorist attacks on New York and the Pentagon in 2001 that erased any ill feeling I had for the nation. I have nothing but admiration for the way the American people came together in the aftermath, and the strength of character they displayed.

Now, as a fully formed adult, rapidly approaching middle age, I am ready to see what Americans are like in all their diversity. I fear their accents and lack of volume control may pain my tender ears, but I am willing to give it a go, if only so that my perceptions of the US are based on facts and not just on stereotypes and prejudices.

Along the way, I hope to fill the void in my head where some details of American history should be and to learn how this former British possession came to be the most powerful nation in the world. I would also like to understand what prompted the miserable old bat, who latched onto me during a beautiful boat ride along the Bosphorus in Istanbul, to declare, 'I could have lived without that. Everything is so much better back home in America.'

NEW YORK

THE EXASPERATED SIGH and lack of movement communicated something was amiss. It was the first week in November and I had just landed in New York; this wasn't the enthusiastic welcome to America I had expected. Another glance at my hotel booking revealed a seemingly inconsequential detail - off 9th Street. It achieved what my first instruction - 147 First Avenue - had failed to do and stirred the cabbie into life.

Darkness was falling as we drove in from the airport and I was struck by the amount of litter lining the roadside. I took it as confirmation of the US' disregard for the environment, finally understanding its refusal to sign up to climate change mitigation targets. As we neared the city, a forest of tower blocks loomed up out of nowhere, the Empire State Building standing proudest of all. Their lights twinkled against the black sky and a shiver of excitement ran through me...I was in New York.

As a stickler for accuracy, I must state that my hotel was physically on 9th Street, off First Avenue. Grappling with nonsensical addresses would be a constant throughout my stay because, either through a lack of history or imagination, the city planners chose to name New York's streets using an absurd system of numbers and compass points.

As someone who struggles to know her left hand from her right, who panics whenever numbers are involved and needs to chant naughty-elephants-squirt-water to work out directions, stepping outside my hotel became an exercise in mental agility.

Exploring New York is like a going on a treasure hunt: you have to decipher codes to find the places you wish to visit. For instance, the address of the disappointingly sparse Guggenheim museum is 1071 Fifth Avenue, off East 89th Street. The museum's actual geographic coordinates (40.7830 degrees north, 73.9590 degrees west) are less confusing.

Just when you think you've got the hang of it, they drop in proper street names to throw you off track. So in between Fifth Avenue and Third Avenue you have Madison Avenue, Park Avenue and Lexington Avenue. As you move in the direction of Downtown, which has traditional style street names thanks to its original Dutch settlers, Park Avenue briefly turns into the missing Fourth Avenue for no discernible reason, and Lexington Avenue changes into Irving Place. It is anarchy.

Once on First Avenue, you might reasonably assume that you have reached the extremity, but you would be mistaken. Instead, the logic-defying system switches from numbers to letters, giving you avenues A, B, C and D.

The city planners should have held a competition to come up with ideas if they were struggling for inspiration. That's what Dubai did when it was looking to name its new fountain, although admittedly the winning entry was Dubai Fountain.

The New York subway adds further layers of complexity to navigating the city. Its lines have colours, numbers and letters to denote where they do and don't go. I made the mistake of asking for directions and the ticket man responded with what sounded like the Enigma code, barked at me in such an unexpectedly strong New York accent that I didn't retain anything he said. But it would have been something like this: 'Take the red line, trains 1,2 or 3 to 14th Street. Change to the yellow line then take trains B, D, F or M to West 4th Street.'

It makes you wonder how many of the city's rough sleepers simply gave up trying to figure out how to get home.

The lack of sensible street names aside, New York is a wonderful metropolis with plenty to occupy a traveller. I am not ashamed to admit that I stuck to the well-beaten tourist trail contained within Manhattan; I was at the start of a great adventure and I thought it would be a shame to get murdered in my first city in America.

I spent a sombre first morning engrossed in the 9/11 museum and memorial, before wandering around the financial district on the look-out for fat cats. On Brooklyn Bridge, a marvel of brick and string engineering completed in 1883, I admired the city spread out before me, while kamikaze cyclists bellowed at me to move out of their way, without breaking speed.

Central Park was exhibiting its autumnal range with infinite varieties of reds, yellows and browns. Kicking up the dried leaves and the occasional camouflaged dog treat, I strolled about half its length to the Jacqueline Onassis Reservoir, which sadly doesn't take the form of her sunglasses. On the return leg, I paused in front of a warmly wrapped jazz ensemble, and a man screamed in my face when I didn't return his greeting.

Times Square is a supersized version of London's Piccadilly Circus. Blindingly bright videos plead with you to consume something…anything - Eat! Drink! Buy! - just spend some money for America's sake! It should be grotesque, but the ultra-high resolution of the television screens makes everything seem desirable, especially the cool, frothy beer at nine thirty in the morning.

Fifth Avenue was crowded with shoppers pushing in opposite directions, wielding fashion house bags as weapons. I may have the distinction of being the only tourist never to have set foot in its famous department stores.

On Ellis Island, home to the portly lady Liberty statue gifted by France and the entry point for millions of migrants to America, I considered what lessons the US' could offer Germany's Angela Merkel, who had just opened her arms to everyone.

Between 1880 and 1924, some 26 million people emigrated to America from across the world, but predominantly from southern and eastern Europe. At first, there was an open-door policy as the newcomers boosted the US' economy, accelerating industrial development and providing labour for the infrastructure projects that built the nation. Support programmes were established to ensure the immigrants quickly assimilated. Later, however, with jobs and housing growing scarce, overcrowding, crime and disease on the rise, resentment surfaced among the population. White supremacist groups reared their ugly heads, broadening their hatred to include Catholics, Jews and immigrants in general; curbs on arrivals soon followed.

When it comes to food on my travels, I live by the mantra 'when in Rome do as the Romans do'. So I made certain to eat only authentic American fare while in New York, which according to the menus meant Philly steak sandwiches, burgers, chicken wings…basically anything involving bread and eating with your fingers. In retrospect, I realise I made a big mistake. Most Romans dine on anything but American food, and with good reason.

The millions of hopefuls that came to start a new life in America carried with them only meagre possessions as they funnelled through Ellis Island, but their heads brimmed with memories of home, including recipes handed down by their parents and grandparents. Food became central to their identity, binding families and communities together, and helping them to remain connected with their heritage.

Enterprising migrants established restaurants to cater to these burgeoning new communities and many still survive today. Their menus have changed little over the last century, even as ownership has passed through the family, and they continue to provide second and third-generation immigrants a treasured link to their roots.

New York's rich and diverse culinary scene is one of the enduring legacies of the mass migration that continued through Ellis Island up until 1954; the locals even claim it to be the gastronomic capital of the world, a boast I quickly rejected on account of the stodge I had been eating. After a lifetime of sausage and sauerkraut, maybe this is the prize that Angela Merkel had set her eye on in welcoming a million migrants to Germany?

Unimpressed by the food I thought New York was offering me, I found pleasure instead in its kaleidoscope of architecture. It is a concrete jungle, as a wise lady once said, yet somehow every building seems distinct, in height, in shape or in colour.

Across Manhattan, Beaux Arts and Art Deco gems compete for attention with their extravagant embellishments or their rectilinear simplicity. No modern edifice has come close to achieving the grace and elegance of the buildings designed between 1880 and 1930, the most well-known examples being the Flatiron, Charles Scribner's Sons and the Rockefeller Center.

The contemporary glass and steel structures shout only of profit, but they too contribute to the disordered New York skyline. They provide the space for the stone masterpieces to breathe and they contrast with the textures of the squat, brick buildings, ensuring that nothing loses its form in the jumble of architectural styles.

Unlike the rambling roads of Europe which tempt you around corner after corner, the streets of New York stretch unending to the horizon. There is always something to draw you on though: an intriguing shop front, a church sandwiched amid symbols of corporate America, or simply a slither of sunlight exploiting a gap between the high rises.

In the residential areas, the fire escapes steal the show. Climbing obtrusively up the brick walls of tenement blocks, they provide a permanent reminder that tragedy can strike at any moment. There is an intangible beauty to these life-saving staircases, each with its unique characteristics. But as much as I grew to love them, I felt it was rather like leaving a ladder against your bedroom window and hoping nobody breaks in.

As I mooched about the tourist sights, I spent an unnecessary amount of time trying to fathom why New York is often labelled the greatest city in the world, and I came to the realisation that even if it were merely the greatest city in America, I had now seen the best the country had to offer. That meant my trip would go downhill from here on in, so perhaps I should have risked a visit to the Bronx after all.

TRAIN 1 - NEW YORK TO BOSTON

IN AN IMMEDIATE deviation from my hastily sketched route around America, I decided to head to Boston from New York. I arrived at the characterless Penn Station1, located near Maddison Square Garden arena, with more than an hour to spare just in case security was tight and to allow plenty of time to find my seat.

But there were neither security checks nor seat allocations, and the platform was announced just seven minutes before the train was due to leave. My orienteering skills were put to the test again as I spun around in search of Track 11 East, and a frantic scramble followed as everyone charged towards the escalator, bags and coats flailing around.

Once onboard, I found the train to be clean and comfortable. I sat in the quiet coach and the lady on the tannoy informed us this meant no sound-emitting devices were permitted and talking had to be kept to a minimum and to a whisper. For the entire three and a half hour journey, I didn't hear a peep. The major stereotype I had accepted of all Americans being shouty and having verbal

---

[1] The original Penn Station, described by *The New York Times* as the Parthenon on steroids, was demolished in the mid-1960s, a mere 50 years after opening.

diarrhoea was well and truly smashed. Had this been a quiet coach in the UK, there would have been music blaring from headphones, various people having loud and inappropriate conversations, and at least one noisy crisp eater.

The only unpleasantness I experienced was the brief waft of an egg sandwich being consumed, which technically was allowed as the lady on the tannoy hadn't specified any rules about obnoxious odours.

My decision to travel around America by train was immediately rewarded with magnificent views of New York as the *Acela Express* trundled across the broad Hudson River, named after the English navigator Henry Hudson, who explored the area on behalf of the Dutch in the early 17th century, leading to the establishment of the New Netherland colony, which later fell into the hands of the British.

It was an overcast day, the sky a blanket of white as we continued through the industrial hinterland of steel plants and storage depots. Before long, we burst into countryside, and for the next few hours I gazed out contentedly at autumnal woodlands. Swollen rivers and marshes frequently sliced through the picture, and timber houses built in the traditional New England style, painted in soft pastels, flashed in and out of view. I questioned the wisdom of having wooden homes in a country famed for its hurricanes and tornados.

The train made brief stops in Stamford and New Haven, after which we were teased with glimpses of sandy beaches as we skirted the Atlantic coast. By the time we crossed the vast bay outside Providence, the capital of Rhode Island, the weather was clearing, and as we moved back inland towards Boston, the landscape became thickly wooded again. Whenever we gathered speed, the train would begin juddering, reminding me of the recent spate of rail accidents in America.

BOSTON

I HAVE ALWAYS ASSOCIATED Boston with being the hometown of the long-haired Nineties rock group Extreme - think timeless classics *More Than Words* and *Get The Funk Out*. Long before I discovered my anti-American convictions, I passed many hours in my bedroom as a young teenager gazing lustfully at posters of the band, desperate to visit Boston to win the heart of either Nuno or Gary, and preferably both. But it turns out handsome middle-aged rockers are not the city's only draw.

Boston was the cradle of the revolution that brought an end to British rule in America in the 18th century and various sites of historical interest are dotted around its centre. I was proud to see a strong imprint of Englishness preserved in old Boston's cobblestone streets and Georgian townhouses, with their sash windows and stately doors; only the occasional wooden interloper belies the terraces from belonging to a well-heeled home counties town.

Boston Common, the US' oldest public park established in 1634, sat between my hotel and the city centre. My mugging anxiety lessened each time I beetled across it and encountered nothing more menacing than dog walkers and ducks lurking among the weeping willows.

It was on Boston Common that thousands of British troops set up camp some 250 years ago as tensions rose between the motherland and her 13 American colonies. London had decided to levy taxes on its settlements along the east coast of America to raise funds following a yet another costly war with France. The colonists, accustomed to governing themselves, objected to the imposition of taxes without prior consultation and by a parliament in which they had no direct representation. Through popular resistance and boycotts, they succeeded in getting certain tax laws repealed, only for them to be replaced soon after with new ones. This toughened their resolve and their acts of rebellion escalated.

The most notorious show of defiance against British authority was the Boston Tea Party of 1773, led by the rebel rouser Samuel Adams, who found greater fame posthumously as a brand of beer. The incident saw the contents of 342 chests of tea tipped into Boston harbour - a man-made ecological disaster that would find echoes in the Gulf of Mexico in 2010.

From the shared sense of injustice, a feeling of a common American identity was forged between the east coast colonies, and London's repeated attempts to clamp down on dissent served only to set them on the path to armed uprising.

There is no accurate record of whether it was King George's men or American militia who fired the first musket in the stand-off at Lexington on the 19th April 1775 that marked the outbreak of war. Either way, it fell on deaf ears as the opening salvo of a second skirmish at Concord later the same day would become known as the 'shot heard around the world'[2] - the shot that would lead to the birth of a new nation and change forever the global balance of power.

Boston was also the setting for the Battle of Bunker Hill in June 1775, a defining moment in the American War of Independence. Although the British redcoats won the encounter,

---

[2] Ralph Waldo Emerson coined the phrase in his poem *Concord Hymn*.

which actually took place on a different hill[3], they suffered twice the number of casualties as the ragtag American army. This boosted the confidence of the inexperienced and outnumbered soldiers, motivating them to push forward with fighting their cause.

Having passed the point of no return, America declared its independence from Britain on the 2nd July 1776, famously establishing 'life, liberty and the pursuit of happiness' as inalienable rights. This momentous event is commemorated two days late every year, on the 4th July. Thomas Jefferson penned the Declaration of Independence while still only 33 years old, however, his most cherished gift to humanity would prove to be the invention of the swivel chair, which centuries later continues to draw inspired thoughts out of browbeaten office workers the world over.

Jefferson was not a lone genius among America's founding fathers: handy-about-the-house Benjamin Franklin is credited with inventing bifocal glasses, a flexible catheter, the lightning rod, a type of stove and the glass armonica. The latter is a musical instrument based on the refined after-dinner pastime of running a licked finger around the rim of a wine glass to elicit sound.

The American War of Independence would only end in 1783, after France and Spain swung the outcome by siding with the now united states, forcing Britain to surrender.

Drinking and eating have replaced revolution as the favourite pastime in Boston. Today, market halls occupy the city centre, their overladen stalls assaulting senses with mouth-watering temptations. I had an obligatory Boston chowder, comforted by a free sample that it would be money well spent - after my New York experiences I was now wary about American food - before heading to the Little Italy district for a main course of pizza. There, on Saturday afternoons, queues snake down the street for a table at the most popular restaurants.

---

[3] American troops were sent to fortify Bunker Hill, but in the dark they confused it with Breed's Hill.

At dusk, I strolled along Commonwealth Avenue, a millionaires' row judging by the ornate staircases, colossal chandeliers and museum-worthy paintings visible through the illuminated, curtainless windows. I somehow resisted the urge to zoom my camera into their monied lives. The adjacent Newbury Street is the place to end the night, flitting between the bustling bars and restaurants in the basements of its red-brick terraced houses, which wouldn't look out of place in a town in northern England.

The following day, before heading to the station, I visited Harvard University, founded by English settlers in 1636. It is situated across Boston's river, which still honours King Charles I, in the small town of Cambridge, named after the British educational establishment opened in 1209.

There, I did what I term a parasite tour, where you amble around within earshot of tour groups, pretending not to be listening, popping up and disappearing at will, and stealing snippets of information along the way.

I learnt that the original writers of the Simpsons met at Harvard, Mark Zuckerberg of Facebook fame and Bill Gates, the philanthropist and computer wizard, both dropped out of the university, while John F Kennedy is one of eight presidents to have studied there. The library was paid for by the family of a former student who drowned with the Titanic.

Most interestingly, George Washington - the man who would be America's first president - used the university as a base for his troops during the War of Independence. His soldiers, being soldiers, burnt the soft furnishings and interior woodwork to keep themselves warm and turned the doorknobs and locks into bullets. After the men moved on, Harvard petitioned the Massachusetts House of Representatives for compensation, and thus began America's love affair with lawsuits.

There is a myth that if visitors rub the left foot of the university's first benefactor, John Harvard, a family member will gain a place at the world-renowned institution. Even though his statue is modelled on someone else, tourists are happy to queue for the opportunity to redirect destiny. I laughed heartily from my vantage point as one after the other they lifted up their progeny to touch the old man's shoe, for there is also a tradition for male students, at the end of their first year, to urinate on that very same foot. My parasitic ears had spared me a humiliation.

TRAIN 2 - BOSTON TO WASHINGTON

WHILE WAITING FOR the overnight train from Boston to Washington, I had my first doubts about what I was doing. Homeless people were circling the station, a constant stream in and out of the toilets; mostly male, but a couple of females too, one chuntering away to herself. I grew apprehensive about what lay in store on the train.

I was going to be travelling along the route where a train had derailed earlier in the year, yet it was a different kind of safety at the forefront of my mind. Visions of frenzied stabbings and violent rapes flashed in my head. I couldn't help but smile broadly at the absurdity of my predicament: I really didn't need to be going through this discomfort and possibly endangering my life. Flying around America would have been too easy, though; everybody does that, no one goes by train. Maybe this is why?

I calmed my nerves by recalling the high cost of train tickets and reminding myself I wasn't waiting for the New York subway. I was travelling on my $686 rail pass, which covers 12 journeys and lasts for a month. Without it, a single ticket to Washington would have cost $184.

The platform was announced 40 minutes before the train was due to depart and I descended the escalator to a dingy underground track, only to retreat after two trains sped through, injecting the trapped air with diesel fumes. Better to sit among malodorous tramps than inhale harmful emissions, I resolved.

The waiting area gradually started to fill with other passengers and we soon outnumbered the homeless. It seems most people don't like to get to the station as early as I do. Before long, we were settled in our comfortable seats on the *Northeast Regional*, ready for the nine-and-a-half-hour train journey ahead. The standard of cleanliness onboard was again impressive, right down to the loos.

Train toilets are often an adventure in themselves. I have done a fair few overnight rail journeys in Russia and while the sleeper carriages are famed for their neatly pressed linen and substantial pillows, the lavatories are squalid. There is no need to ask where they are, you just follow your nose.

Before entering a Russian train loo, I always try to take a deep enough breath to see me through my full bodily motion. The door, for reasons unknown, is designed to slam shut behind you like an animal trap, preventing the circulation of fresh air. The metallic washbasin and toilet bowl suggest clinical cleanliness, but the burn in your nostrils tells otherwise. The stench of stale urine is so strong it coats your tongue.

I don't know what people get up to in there. I assume for drunk Russian men, trying to aim into a toilet bowl while being thrown around on a train is like trying to control a fire hose. With an eye to health and safety, the railway authorities put down non-slip shower mats to stop you skidding over in the slosh (there can be no stains on their conscience). The drill for Russian train toilets is to unload and get out as soon as possible.

In parts of Asia, the trains are fitted with squat toilets. You can do what you like in those, there are no rules. No one would even notice if you did a dirty protest. The big question is where to put your bag while you go about your business. Certainly, the hook, if ever there was one, will have broken decades ago. The floor never has any dry areas, and the sinks are usually crying tears of spittle. If you keep your rucksack on your back, you risk falling over like a turtle when the train slams into a bend. So what do you do? This is what is known as a third-world problem.

The challenge is altogether different on modern British trains: it is about dropping your luggage before someone opens the door and catches you exposing yourself. Even though it has never happened to you, and maybe has never happened to anyone, the fear is very real. It stems from the fact that the door is considerably further than an arm's length away from the toilet seat and its locking mechanism inspires no confidence.

Rather than a reassuringly solid bolt or latch, there is an electric button to close and open the door, which, to enable wheelchair access, sweeps wide open and disappears into the wall, revealing the entire water closet to whomever happens to be hanging around. You can never be sure whether the automatic lock has worked, yet you know for certain that the second the door closes someone will be jabbing the button impatiently to get in. Prayers are said as you gingerly lower your knickers. *Please don't let the door open.*

The same thoughts always play through your mind as you hover over the soiled toilet seat. First, you try to work out how many steps you would need to take with your pants down and arm outstretched to reach the door and block the entrance of an intruder. Calculations done, you then remind yourself that this defensive move would be fruitless in any case because you can't override the electronic system once the door starts opening. Better to stay put and smile at your audience, you conclude for the umpteenth time, before finishing up and leaving relieved, in both senses of the word.

Happily, I can report no issues whatsoever with the train toilets in America. They were always clean, well-stocked with paper and easy on the nose. A reflection of the railway staff or the users? I would say probably both.

My first overnight train journey in the US also passed off peacefully and without incident. No one spoke a word, except for an Englishman who made a call home to his wife.

WASHINGTON

IT ALWAYS ASTOUNDS me that whenever I say the geographic name Washington every American feels the need to clarify which one I mean. I just don't understand how it isn't immediately obvious that I am referring to their nation's capital, rather than a far-flung northwestern state of the same name or one of dozens of obscure towns, villages and cities called Washington that I have certainly never heard of. For me, Washington is just Washington. To add the D.C., seems so, well, American. But to avoid any ambiguity, I would like to explicitly state that this chapter concerns, in its entirety, the political centre of the United States.

Compared with New York's 8.5 million people, Washington is a thinly populated city of less than 700,000. I exited Union Station at about half past seven in the morning; my taxi swept past lines of homeless people waiting for food handouts. Many others in the prime of their lives lurked on street corners, reminding me of the wasted potential I had seen in South Africa. I was dropped off at a hotel sandwiched between two derelict buildings. It was an inauspicious start, and I felt on edge, for I was only too aware that Washington is the murder capital of America.

Hotels in the US have ridiculously late check-in times, in addition to hidden fees and taxes, which inflate the price beyond recognition when you come to pay. The check-in time for my Washington hotel was four o'clock, so all I could do was dump my bag and venture out to explore in yesterday's clothes.

An initial study of the map threw me into panic. It seemed even more complex than New York, with a combination of state names, letters, numbers and compass points used to identify the streets. The address of my hotel was 933 L Street NW, if you can call that an address.

The Lonely Planet guidebook gives the following account of how it works: 'The city was designed by its two planners to be perfectly navigable. Unfortunately, their urban visions have mashed up against each other. Pierre L'Enfant's diagonal state-named streets share space with Andrew Ellicott's grid - remember letters go east-west, numbers north-south. On top of that, the city is divided into four quadrants with identical addresses in different divisions.'

Clear as mud.

Against all expectations, the system proved itself to be quite logical. The street signs even indicate which numbers are in each block, a practical arrangement that New York would do well to adopt.

I sensed myself relaxing as the city started to fill up with office workers arriving from their commute. Washington is remarkably clean and orderly. The area was chosen in 1790 to be the site of a purpose-built capital for the young republic. A second phase of development occurred in the 1930s, during which more government buildings were erected and wooden boarding houses were removed, gentrifying the heart of the city. Still today, there is an air of artificiality about the place. It lacks the randomness of cities that have evolved in tandem with architectural trends; there is none of the grit and character of New York.

Far from being sterile, it is an imposing city - just as its planners intended. They wanted to create a capital city worthy of an aspiring global power and sought inspiration from around the world when designing its public buildings, monuments and open spaces. Most of the structures are neoclassical in style, making Washington appear oddly familiar to a European traveller. The sore thumb sticking out is the FBI headquarters, a brutalist monstrosity dating from the 1970s.

Washington is, in essence, a city of federal offices and museums. About 20 museums have been established thanks to an English scientist, who wanted to immortalise his name. When James Smithson died in 1829, he left a half-million-dollar endowment to fund an institution in Washington for 'the increase and diffusion of knowledge', even though he had never visited the United States. Our loss was America's gain. The Smithsonian Institution museums are free to enter, and it would take weeks to do justice to their extraordinarily rich collections.

The National Air & Space Museum, for instance, includes the Wright Brothers' plane that achieved the first recorded flight in 1903; the Spirit of St Louis in which Charles Lindbergh completed the first nonstop solo transatlantic flight from New York to Paris in 1927 in 33.5 hours; and more modern exhibits such as Steve Fossett's balloon and Spaceship One.

The pride of Washington, however, is the softly lit rotunda in the National Archives Museum, where the country's most important historical documents - the Declaration of Independence, the Constitution and the Bill of Rights - are displayed.

After issuing the Declaration of Independence in 1776, America's founding fathers continued to roll out the paperwork. The Articles of the Confederation were agreed in 1781, under which the 13 former British colonies banded into a perpetual union of self-governing states. However, it quickly became obvious the national government (Congress) had been left with no authority over the states, so the Constitution was written to replace the Articles, establishing the executive branch of government (President) and giving the federal government the power to tax, spend and regulate interstate commerce. The Constitution was approved in 1788, and the Bill of Rights, a list of amendments to the Constitution intended to protect individual freedoms from tyrannical government, was ratified in 1789, the same year that George Washington was sworn in as America's first president in the temporary capital New York.

Having followed the independence trail around Boston and stood by the broken slab, making the spot where Washington gave his inaugural presidential address, and now seeing before me the so-called Freedom Documents, I felt I was starting to grasp something of the American psyche.

Whereas previously I rejected all claims of America inventing democracy and being the greatest nation in the world as pure arrogance and hubris, I could now at least appreciate the basis for these false assertions. I understood that America was the first country to win independence from the British Empire, establishing in place of a monarchy a unique model of governance, and little more than 150 years after going it alone, it succeeded in becoming the world's largest economic power. These are quite some achievements and I concluded that maybe they are reason enough for the overwhelming self-belief that Americans possess and their inability to whisper.

Strength of national pride is one of the defining characteristics of Americans, although it has been tinged a little with embarrassment since Trump began tweeting from the White House. This immense patriotism stems in no small part from the fact that generations of American children have begun their school day by pledging allegiance to the US flag and 'to the republic for which it stands, one nation under God, indivisible, with liberty and justice for all.' While it may sound a bit Hitler youth, such rituals have proven important in forging a sense of national identity in a country built mostly through immigration. The migrants lacked a shared ancestry and so the founding ideals of the United States provided the common bond, uniting people of diverse ethnicities and becoming central to American identity. This explains their love of the Constitution and their wont to overuse the word liberty.

The main sights in Washington are set along a nearly two-mile-long strip of land known as the National Mall, which runs from the US Capitol, the seat of the legislative branch of the federal government, down to the Potomac river. The area around the river is given over to memorials of presidents and wars.

The Lincoln Memorial, modelled on the Parthenon in Athens, identifies Abraham Lincoln as America's favourite president and one that bears an uncanny resemblance to Roald Dahl's BFG. But it is at the understated exhibition in the Ford Theatre where you get the true sense of the man.

The exhibition charts the American Civil War that began in 1861 shortly after Lincoln's election, and the days leading up the shooting of the president in the theatre by John Wilkes Booth in April 1865, just days after the war officially ended.

That cold-blooded act launched another great American tradition: presidential assassinations. To date, four US presidents have been slain in office: the 16th (Lincoln), 20th (James A Garfield), 25th (William McKinley) and 35th (John F Kennedy), while about a dozen others have survived attempts on their lives.

It was the issue of slavery that divided America and plunged it into civil war. Although the Constitution was purposely ambiguous on the topic as many of the founding fathers were themselves slave owners, the industrialising northern states, enamoured with capitalist ideology, recognised that slavery didn't sit with the country's founding ideals, so they gradually outlawed it, with New Jersey the last state to do so in 1804.

The US banned international slave trading in 1808 and the newly enlightened British abolished slavery throughout the Empire in 1833, but slave ownership was still legal in all 15 southern states of America at the start of the 1860s.

As debate intensified over the morality and legality of slavery, southerners began to fear financial ruin: their vast cotton, sugar and tobacco plantations were entirely built on slave labour.

The question of the extension of slavery into new territories acquired from Mexico[4] became the flashpoint between the pro-

---

[4] California, Nevada, Utah, and parts of Arizona, New Mexico, Colorado and Wyoming joined the United States following the 1846-48 Mexican-American War - see San Antonio chapter.

slavery south and anti-slavery north, with both sides concerned their influence in Congress would be diluted as the federation expanded.

The final straw would prove to be Lincoln's success in the November 1860 presidential election. Lincoln represented the newly formed Republican party and gained a reputation with his anti-slavery campaign speeches. He won the election without any electoral votes from the south and the slave states took this as confirmation of their exclusion from the political system.

Before Lincoln even moved into the White House, seven southern states had seceded from the United States of America (the Union) to form the Confederate States of America, and four more states would join them.

The Confederates fired the first shots in the Civil War that inevitably followed, taking Fort Sumter in Charleston harbour in April 1861. But it would be the 23 northern states that would emerge victorious in 1865, after nearly 620,000 lives had been taken - about 2 per cent of the population of America at the time.

The decisive moment in the conflict was Lincoln's proclamation freeing all the slaves in the Confederacy. This helped the Union to victory by depriving the rebel states of the manpower behind their war effort; the 1863 Emancipation Proclamation would also wreck the economy of the south and have profound social consequences. The Confederates agreed a surrender at Appomattox on 9 April 1865; six days later, Lincoln was dead.

The Ford Theatre museum in Washington tells how Lincoln had a premonition of his assassination, and follows the manhunt after his murder. Lincoln's portrayal as a hardworking, selfless family man, who met his death just a month after being re-elected as president, together with his ultimate legacy - the abolition of slavery in America - make it understandable why he is still so revered today. However, Lincoln was not the die-hard abolitionist that history has made him and there are moments in his speeches that would be classified as racist by today's standards.

And this is where America's claims to a moral high ground fall down. The Declaration of Independence was based on the premise of all men being created equal and endowed by God with certain unalienable rights including life, liberty and the pursuit of happiness. Yet from the very outset, the new country failed to live up to these ideals. America's great experiment with democracy was also a great experiment with hypocrisy, for these unalienable rights extended only to white men.

While the United States presented itself as the beacon of liberty and freedom in the world, slavery was allowed to continue for nearly another hundred years. Where was liberty in the Fugitive Slave Act of 1850, which criminalised anyone who helped an escaped slave? The Capitol building, the very symbol of American independence and republicanism, was constructed using slave labour. A century after slavery was belatedly abolished, Martin Luther King would still have to stand on the steps of Lincoln's vast marble memorial to demand civil rights for blacks following decades of segregation. Women too were marginalised in society and excluded from the political system. Attempts were made to wipe out the Native Americans. And the list continues. This was no utopia.

A myth of exceptionalism has been woven throughout American history. With the eyes of the world upon them, politicians and commentators have allowed themselves to be led by a sense of occasion, flavouring their rhetoric with weighty refrains such as 'the city on a hill', 'manifest destiny' and 'the last best hope of earth'. They have helped to shape the idea of America being a model society, destined to occupy the land between the Atlantic and the Pacific, and chosen by God to take democracy to the undemocratic world. The greatest nation on earth.

Their version of history conveniently settles on the Pilgrim fathers as origins of America, rather than the debauched Jamestown colonists and the Spanish and Dutch explorers that preceded them, or indeed the Native Americans that inhabited the land first. Their version of history frames the American Revolution around the lofty ideals of freedom and self-determination when it was actually rooted in money. Their version of history ignores the horrors of slavery and segregation, the obvious flaws in America's system of governance and the mirage of the American dream. Their version of history overlooks the fact that rather than charting a unique path, Washington followed the European powers into imperial adventures and equally unjustifiable wars to further the interests of a powerful business elite. Only today is America's distorted origin story beginning to unravel and with it the country's misplaced sense of superiority and bogus claims of moral leadership.

Despite its abysmal crime statistics, Washington felt very safe as I meandered from the Capitol down to the White House, where Christmas tree decorating was in full swing under the watchful gaze of snipers prowling the roof. I was disappointed by the absence of tinsel, which regretfully seems to have fallen out of favour the world over, but the presence of officers with secret service written on their uniforms filled me with seasonal cheer.

With several months of pre-planning, it is possible to get approval to tour parts of the White House. For those of us who are less organised, there is a nearby visitor centre, which explains the evolution of the president's home. It is thanks to us British that the White House got its name. During the War of 1812[5], informally known as America's Second War of Independence and Half-arsed Attempt to Steal Canada, we set fire to all the public buildings in Washington as revenge for the United States torching public and private property in Canada. When the presidential pad was restored, it was painted white and the rest, as they say, is history.

The White House forms part of a national park, which means the staff in the visitor centre wear the quintessentially American park ranger outfit. This is basically a 1950s-style scout uniform, of dark green and grey, topped off with a broad brimmed hat. The helpful scout look could not appear more out of place in the global powerhouse that is central Washington.

The exhibition in the visitor centre includes a patriotic video of former presidents and their families discussing their time as

---

[5] This is covered in the New Orleans chapter.

residents of 1,600 Pennsylvania Avenue. They enthuse about what an honour it is to lead the nation, each taking their turn to repeat Lincoln's motto 'government of the people by the people for the people' and to reiterate how after leaving office they simply become one of the masses again. It is a brainwashing experience to hear them and you quickly get sucked into the emotion of it all: Bill Clinton recounting how he and Hillary were too excited sleep on their first night in the White House so they went around exploring all the rooms; Michelle Obama saying it was a new experience for her (duh!), but the White House immediately felt like home; along with appearances from the Carter and Bush clans.

Once the video ends, the bubble bursts and you quickly recall all the self-interest, the indisputable fact that power corrupts and, of course, dear old Bill dishonouring his wife in the Oval Room. This is not a euphemism.

Clinton is just one among many philandering presidents - men considered capable of running a powerful country yet unable to restrain their animal instincts in the presence of the supposed weaker species. The one to beat is Warren Harding, famed for his erotic poetry, paying hush money to lovers and illegitimate children, his penchant for bonking in a cupboard in the White House, and, most notably, his all American phallus, which, letters attest, went by the name of Jerry.

TRAIN 3 – WASHINGTON TO CHICAGO

THE TRAIN FOR Chicago left Washington at five minutes past four, which afforded an hour or so of daylight at the start of the nearly 18-hour journey.

I based myself in the observation carriage as much to enjoy the woodland scenery slipping past the windows as to get away from the woman I was sharing my seat with - literally sharing my seat with. As a rotund lady myself, I can say she was enormous, and she polished off a lasagne before the train even left the station.

The *Capitol Limited* gathered together a microcosm of American society. There was every shape, size and skin tone imaginable as well as several Amish families onboard. They were interesting to study in their hats and bonnets, with their old-fashioned suitcases, wicker picnic baskets and, erm, trainers. Why is it when a religious community eschews modern fashions they always make an exception for trainers? Like the nuns, I suppose the Amish must value corn-free feet over convention.

As I surveyed the handsome boys with their curls and the old-before-their-time girls, I wondered whether they harboured secret thoughts of rebellion, of running away to the city and, heaven forbid, using deodorant. Maybe they really are content to settle for their preordained lives as generations have before them. Maybe there is comfort and freedom in that. Personally, I find the thought *this is it for the rest of my life* terrifying and that is what pushes me to constantly seek challenge and change. But perhaps I just haven't found my life's purpose yet.

Seeing the Amish families going about their lives made me appreciate how welcoming Americans are of diversity, and how intolerant British people can be. In my mind's eye, I could picture only too easily the abuse an Amish family might receive on a train journey in the UK.

As you travel westwards across America, the people become noticeably friendlier and it wasn't long before conversations between strangers were sparking up all around. My first train encounter was with a Palestinian, who had been in the US for a couple of months and was trying to make a new life for himself. Things hadn't worked out in the first city he had chosen, so now he was going to try his hand in Chicago.

He sat down next to me and promptly began crying. He was scared, he said, and didn't know anyone in America. I am not very warm with strangers at the best of times because you have no idea what their intentions are or whether they are honest people, so his tears didn't wash with me. But I was even less sympathetic when he revealed we were the same age.

Here he was, a 39-year-old man, crying to a stranger on a train. A stranger who was travelling around the US alone and yet wasn't afraid; a stranger who has also made fresh starts in various countries during her life. He had chosen the wrong audience.

I tersely told him he should see it as an adventure and if it was meant to be, it would work out alright. I suspected all along he had ulterior motives for speaking to me and true to stereotype, he soon began quizzing me about my personal life, beginning broad before asking the only question he really wanted the answer to. 'Are you single?'

He said he wanted to buy me breakfast or dinner in Chicago. I assumed he meant both, followed again by breakfast. Despite his

Arab good looks, I showed no enthusiasm and, thankfully, the distraction of two men entering the observation car saved me from any further bother. He immediately seized on them to discuss his plight anew, welling up at appropriate moments.

After receiving his fill of advice and sympathy, he returned to his seat in the main carriage. Moments later, the lasagne lady passed through the observation car.

'You don't need to hide out here,' she said, gripping my shoulder with a clammy hand. 'Come and get some rest.' I had been rumbled.

I left it another hour before I reluctantly ventured back, dreading a restless night sat squished alongside her. The money I was saving by not booking sleeper coaches no longer seemed so significant. But as luck would have it, I discovered her seated next to the weeping Palestinian. His arm was hooked around her bulky frame at an awkward angle and stretched to the point of dislocation.

It was a result for me on both scores. Shortly before we reached Chicago, she rang someone to say she was going for breakfast with her new friend. Men are so very fickle.

CHICAGO

THE ONLY RESEARCH I did before leaving for America was to Google crime statistics. As I habitually do with medical symptoms, I kept digging until I found things to terrify me. This meant I was on high alert whenever I arrived in a new city, and I was particularly concerned about Chicago as it is the gun capital of the US.

As with other places, I needn't have fretted so much, especially because many shops and restaurants in Chicago display 'no guns allowed' signs on their doors. I couldn't fail to be comforted by these signs as they undoubtedly act as a strong deterrent to the ill-intentioned.

Actually, I found Chicago to be a very relaxed city, clean and compact enough to explore by foot. It was only when I ventured into the network of creepy underground streets in search of a celebrated drinking hole that I sensed my life was in danger. But reduced levels of oxygen and a lack of escape routes tend to have that effect on me.

A river and an elevated railway weave through the commercial centre, which sits alongside the vast Lake Michigan, one of five Great Lakes in North America. The lake is responsible for the icy wind that blows through your bones in winter, bending you double. It was also responsible for my two days of severely loose stools while in Chicago. Untreated sewage effluent, I belatedly learnt, is regularly dumped into the lake, so the vaguely named 'white fish from Lake Michigan' is best avoided.

Chicago is famed for being the birthplace of the skyscraper. In 1871, a great fire destroyed most of the city centre, leaving 300 people dead and 100,000 homeless. It was decided to rebuild the downtown area using brick and steel, instead of wood. This enabled the construction of much taller buildings. William Le Baron Jenney is credited with inspiring the skyscraper with his 10-storey high Home Insurance Building, which opened in 1885. It used a steel frame and the walls hung from that, rather than fulfilling their traditional role of providing structural support. The Chicago School of Architecture went on to influence city design throughout America and beyond, transforming skylines the world over.

An architecture tour is time well spent in Chicago. As a tourist, you usually admire buildings from the outside, but these take you in to see stunning Art Deco foyers, barely changed since the 1920s. Afterwards, I continued popping into random buildings for shelter from the artic wind and to test the vigilance of the city's security guards.

Chicago's main allure, however, is the legend of the serial entrepreneur, Alphonse Capone. My guidebook detailed a few places where tourists could walk in his bloodstains, but recalling the hours I spent in Berlin searching in vain for vestiges of Hitler's bunker, I decided not to head out alone and signed up for a tacky gangster tour instead.

There really wasn't much to see as over the years the city authorities have done their best to remove any traces of Chicago's most famous resident. There was one bullet hole, a few shopfronts, a hotel, a dance hall and some former speakeasies. The guides, nevertheless, succeeded in bringing to life the Prohibition era that spawned the organised crime syndicates, aided by regular bursts of recorded machine-gun fire, which alarmingly failed to turn heads in central Chicago on a Monday morning.

From 1920 until 1933, the sale, production and distribution of alcohol (although not the consumption of it) was prohibited in America under the 18th amendment to the Constitution, following decades of lobbying by evangelists and women's groups. It was hoped the so-called 'Nobel Experiment' would cut crime rates in cities swollen by immigration and help to restore traditional family values. The opposite happened.

As the alcohol trade was driven underground, anyone wanting a little libation other than during holy communion was pushed into the arms of bootleggers and racketeers. Where legal taverns and bars once quenched the thirst of the nation, illegal speakeasies run by the mafia arrived to plug the gap. Gambling dens and brothels also proliferated.

It was the Roaring Twenties, a time of great prosperity and consumerism; the organised crime bosses were seen as benefactors, risking their freedom to give the people what they wanted. Members of the press, the police and the political establishment - many of whom opposed Prohibition - went on the take, providing advance warnings of raids and helping criminal investigations to be dropped. As the stakes became higher, deadly rivalries broke out between mafia groups.

At the height of Prohibition, it is estimated Al Capone, the most notorious and charismatic gangster - and the most brutal - was racking in more than a $100m a year. He earned himself a reputation as a modern-day Robin Hood by being generous with his money, opening one of the first soup kitchens during the Great Depression and covering tuition fees and healthcare costs for those without the means to do so.

In 1926, the jazz pianist Fats Waller was kidnapped and forced to play at Capone's 27th birthday party, which lasted for three days. When the musician was finally allowed to leave, he took home thousands of dollars in tips. That's mobsterism with a human face.

An administrative oversight would end Capone's glittering career (body count notwithstanding): in November 1931, he was sentenced to 11 years in prison for not filing his tax returns.

'The income tax law is a lot of bunk,' Capone reportedly said at some point. 'The government can't collect legal taxes from illegal money.' There's a life lesson there, if ever there was one.

The 'Noble Experiment' had been a resounding failure. Not only had Prohibition proven disastrous for the American economy[6], which plunged into the Great Depression in 1929, thousands had died from drinking toxic moonshine, gambling and drinking dens were doing a brisker trade than ever, and footfall at knocking shops showed no indication of a return to family values.

In 1933, an amendment to the Constitution was revoked for the first time. The 21st amendment repealed the 18th and put an end to Prohibition.

Trying to spot bullet holes from gangland killings might seem an odd way to spend a morning, but it is quite a tame pastime for Chicago. For more than a century, one of the top things to do in the Windy City was an excursion to the Union Stockyard slaughterhouse.

The stockyard was a vast and bloody operation. At its peak, it employed 40,000 people and 'processed' 19 million animals every year, providing America with 80 per cent of its meat. Viewing galleries allowed visitors to watch the animals having their throats slit, before moving along the 'disassembly' line to see the carcasses stripped and butchered into pieces. No such family fun exists today, though.

*   *   *

It was at this point in my journey that I decided I needed to get my head around the coin situation. As already evidenced in their choice of street names, Americans like to overcomplicate things. When it comes to money, they are no different.

Take the one dollar, for example. It comes in three different formats. Yes, three. There is the one dollar note (or bill as they say in the local lingo), the one dollar brass coin, and the one dollar

---

[6] It is estimated $11bn-worth of tax revenues were lost during Prohibition.

silver coin. The latter is a rare find, I was told, although I had gathered three of them already.

And if that wasn't confusing enough, most of the coins don't display their actual value, they just bear a name meaningless to the outsider like nickel, dime and penny. Meanwhile, the quarter looks identical to the not-so-rare-as-people-claim one dollar silver coin.

I had abandoned using coins in protest at the lack of clarity, but after becoming weighed down with shrapnel, I was pushed to Google for an explanation. It seems a dime is worth ten cents, a nickel is five cents and a penny is worth one cent. The penny, I proudly discovered, is a hangover from British rule. As for the etymology of buck, used today to refer to dollars in general, one disputed theory is it stems from the time when deer hides, or buckskins, were traded between Native Americans and European settlers. So that was the money understood in theory, now I just had to learn to distinguish the coins while under pressure from impatient servers.

TRAIN 4 – CHICAGO TO SAN FRANCISCO

THE CALIFORNIA ZEPHYR is the best-known train journey in America, and one that every rail enthusiast aspires to undertake due to its breathtaking scenery. It connects Chicago with San Francisco, covering the 2,500 miles in about 52 hours. By contrast, a flight between the two cities takes a little over four hours.

The silver-grey, double-decker train pulled out of Chicago at two in the afternoon, and it wasn't long before the shadows outside began lengthening. We made stops at Mendota, Galesburg and other unremarkable pinpoints on the map, and whenever the conductor gave the go ahead, passengers piled off the train for a smoke. At Burlington, we crossed the Mississippi River, which once marked the western boundary of the United States, and after a slow-burning, crimson sunset there was nothing left to admire other than my reflection in the window.

As a long evening stretched ahead, I decided to treat myself to dinner, and wandered along to the restaurant. I had read it is customary for people to be seated with strangers at mealtimes on the *California Zephyr,* so I was apprehensive about my potential blind date.

My heart lifted when I saw the dining car was empty except for a handful of people, and it sank just as rapidly as I was steered towards a table already accommodating a couple in their 50s. Why dirty an empty table when you can deny someone the pleasure of their own company instead?

After an awkward exchange of introductions, the couple encouraged me to order the steak. 'Everybody has the steak on the *California Zephyr,*' I was informed. Even though it cost way more than I had mentally budgeted, I sensed a long perusal of the alternative options would be inappropriate, so I accepted their choice of dinner for me. Our orders were taken together as though we were a group of friends. I worried we might be given a breadbasket to share with one brown roll and two white ones.

The couple were headed to a funeral. They said they were done with flying after nearly dying in a storm on the way to Las Vegas. On subsequent trains, I would also meet people going to funerals, which suggests the grieving process in America involves travelling on the slowest form of transport.

The expensive steak they had chosen for me was underwhelming, but I graciously echoed their compliments while chewing through the dried out flesh. Anyone who manages to cook food on a moving train only deserves praise since I struggle to walk to the toilet without falling over.

Our conversation turned to politics after I recounted my visit to the World Trade Centre memorial and explained how the terror attacks had changed my perception of Americans.

'People hate us because of what our government does, but they need to remember most of us hate our government too,' the man said. For the first time, the possibility entered my head that the average Joe didn't share Washington's desire to dictate how the rest of the world should behave.

It being November 2015, the headlines were dominated by the presidential candidate race and I asked what they thought of Donald Trump. Trump would be good for business was their unanimous response, and he would control the budget well. That threw me: these intelligent people were actually taking him seriously. Clearly, he wasn't participating just for entertainment as I had thought.

We said goodnight and as I bedded down in my chair, I kicked myself for repeating their parting words of 'enjoy the rest of your holiday'. I had forgotten they were going to a funeral. I decided then not to bother with restaurant meals again – it was an unnecessary extravagance.

I slept well until the woman behind started playing a podcast without using headphones. I have no tolerance for other people's noise and I immediately put myself in a rage, cursing her under my breath, and slamming back and forth in my seat. She was oblivious to my wrath even when I got up and glared at her, my overreaction disturbing me far more than her podcast.

She was eventually silenced by an acquaintance who made an unwelcome pass at her. The woman moved place and, after a loud conversation with her mother, finally drifted off to sleep. She was to become a dominant character on the train, orchestrating the smokers and sinking a lot of beer.

I woke somewhere in Nebraska and was treated to a sky crowded with stars. The first light of dawn was breaking on the horizon and there was snow on the ground. I was eager for what lay ahead. During the night, the time zone had changed from Central to Mountain time. It would change again to Pacific time before we reached our destination, the one journey taking us through three of the four time zones in the US mainland, the other being Eastern time.

It tends to be the old men who rise early on the trains, and a handful were already clustered in the observation carriage when I made my way there shortly after the sun was up. I sat on the opposite side to them. It was a wise move because one of them quickly made known that he was 'LDS' - a Mormon. I wondered if he travelled by train as a way of ensuring a captive audience.

Later, with no other seats available, a young girl sat down next to him. He straightaway told her he belonged to a proselytising church; she fell into his trap and asked what that meant. Their discussions over the next few hours brought many a curl to my lips, and I was struck by the interest and patience shown by the girl.

'We celebrate Jesus' life, not his death. Do you think if Jesus had been killed by the guillotine people would wear guillotines round their necks? The cross is just a means of capital punishment.' He had a point.

When you read into the history of the Church of the Latter Day Saints it is a wonder anyone buys into it, though. The basis of the religion is some sheets of gold inscribed with ancient Egyptian texts that were revealed to a poor, lustful farmer from Vermont, who by some miracle was able to translate them into the Book of Mormon. He quickly built up a following so devout that one of his co-founders would become husband to more than 70 women.

That a new religion had been revealed in the early 19th century in the US fitted the belief of many Americans at the time that theirs was the country most beloved by God. People wanted it to be true, and the prophets gladly made sure of it, using whatever means fair or foul. Over the years, the religion has survived a multitude of scandals, as well as persecution, to become an established part of American society.

Mormons are no longer so promiscuous, but they still shun tea, coffee and alcohol, and believe that the Garden of Eden was in Missouri and Noah's ark floated down the Mississippi.

At half past ten, we stopped for an hour in Denver, which boasts a refinery and is a centre for livestock production. The windows got a clean during the break, ahead of the spectacular show of scenery that would follow and leave me spellbound at times, beginning with the various canyons that form the Rocky Mountains. Rivers and streams gushed along the valley floors, through the grasses and past the trees populating the empty lands. Banks of rich, red earth within touching distance of the train offered lessons in geology. Above, the sky was the clearest blue.

For rail enthusiasts, one of the highlights of the journey is the six-mile-long Moffat tunnel, which cuts through the Continental Divide, the mountain ridge that runs from Alaska all the way to the southern tip of Chile. Before the tunnel opened in 1928, trains took five hours to cross the mountains. Today, the *California Zephyr* nips through the tunnel in nine minutes.

We emerged into a snowy mountainscape and soon after stopped at the ski resort of Fraser, the highest railway station in the US. I scrambled off the train to throw some snowballs and inhale the fresh, icy air, while the addicts took in some more carbon monoxide.

From Fraser, the train hugged the powerful Colorado River, weaving its way through picture-book scenery. Occasionally, I experienced view envy, but for most of the journey the floor to ceiling windows on both sides of the train staged an equally impressive show. At half past eleven, an America by Rail tour group clambered onboard and livened things up. They got straight on the rum and cokes, saying it must be four in the afternoon somewhere. I wasn't sure what hotel check-in times had to do with anything.

We passed an area famous for hot sulphur springs. Autumn was only just getting under way in Colorado, much later than on the east coast - a reminder, if a 52-hour train ride was not enough, of the vastness of America.

Once we crossed into Utah, the landscape became even more dramatic. In one moment, we feasted our eyes on red, weather-worn rock formations, in the next, soaring snow-capped mountains. Then after rounding a corner, the land would fall away to complete flatness. This was America's wild west.

Although the train would often fall hours behind schedule, somehow it managed to reach all the major stops on time, if not early. At about eleven o'clock at night, we rolled into Salt Lake City, and I got to save the day as the Mormon and his convert failed to notice it was their stop. I helped to gather her scattered belongings (why do some people do that on trains?) and they leapt off just in the nick of time.

I had decided against visiting the city because the train arrived too late for me as a lone female traveller. When the conductor warned the smokers not to wander outside the station as it wasn't safe, I gave myself a pat on the back for my wise caution.

The Salar de Uyuni salt lake in Bolivia had been a highlight of my Latin American travels a few years earlier. It entailed a gruelling three-day road trip, sleeping in freezing cold accommodation without electricity and hot water, all while suffering the effects of altitude sickness. But our efforts were rewarded with an unforgettable sunrise over an eerie, dazzling white, lunar-like expanse that stretched as far as the eye could see. Pressing my nose against the train window, I convinced myself I could see Utah's salt flats through the darkness.

We were in snowy Nevada when I woke from my uncomfortable slumber, and I quickly made my way to the observation carriage to bag a prime position. That means somewhere in the middle, with a socket, a table and no companions.

It wasn't long before a guy wearing flipflops attached himself to me. He was a seasonal worker returning home after a spell away packing potatoes. For the rest of the day, I had to endure his hairy, crossover toes wiggling away in my peripheral vision, his feet raised on a ledge far closer to my face than should be legal.

Not content with ruining my enjoyment of one of the world's most scenic train rides with his toey presence, he also proceeded to whinge incessantly. He wanted the journey to end. It was his first time on a train and he hated it. He couldn't see why anyone would want to travel by train. He vowed he would never do so again. Ad nauseam.

I don't understand how some people fail to be moved by the beauty of the natural world around us, but I have noticed they tend to be the same folks who have music permanently blearing in their ears. It is as if they are afraid to be alone with their thoughts. I have never owned a Walkman or an iPod. I have always been content to gaze for hours out of a window, quietly absorbed in my contemplations, or often not thinking at all, just watching the world go by. There is no better pastime than staring through a moving window, except perhaps beer tasting or sucking on crisps to make them last longer.

I suppose he couldn't appreciate the beauty of what we were travelling through in the same way he couldn't appreciate that male toes should never be on public view.

On the third and final day on the train, we saw mudflats and heard explanations from a railway museum guide, who joined us at the casino town of Reno. He recounted, in his strong Californian drawl, the construction of the first trans-America railway.

In 1862, Abraham Lincoln commissioned two private railroad companies to build the so-called Transcontinental line. Union Pacific, financed by the appropriately named George Francis Train, began construction of the railway near the Missouri River and worked westwards, while Central Pacific, whose backers included Leland Stanford, later of university fame, began near the Sacramento River in California and worked eastwards. After a faltering start, the two firms raced against each other to trigger maximum payment bonuses for the amount of track laid.

The railway was completed in 1869, a few years after the end of the Civil War, and it helped to bind America back together as one nation, uniting the country physically from the Atlantic Ocean to the Pacific. It also opened up vast lands to be settled, and dozens of towns would spring up along its route in the years that followed. By 1883, three other cross-country lines had been constructed.

In the snowy mountains around Truckee, the *California Zephyr* has a speed limit of 30 miles an hour - a perfect pace for taking in the views of Lake Tahoe, sat among the pine trees. Here, the railway museum guide shared a gruesome story about a group of settlers, whose westward-bound wagon convoy ran into difficulty in the area in 1846. Early snowfall trapped the already hungry and exhausted travellers in the Sierra Nevada Mountains. Faced with starvation, they resorted to eating boiled horse bones, mice and even ox hide rugs and shoelaces, before finally turning to cannibalism to survive. It took five months for rescuers to reach them; just 48 members of the original party of 87 made it to California.

As we drew nearer to Sacramento, the state capital of California, signs of civilisation returned, and I saw homeless people sheltering under trees in make-shift houses. The train stopped in Emeryville and from there, I took a shuttle bus to San Francisco, at last within grasp of a shower and a bed after three days on the move.

SAN FRANCISCO

I OFTEN GET A BAD first impression of a place that later proves to be unfounded. The same is true of people. I draw hasty conclusions based on initial appearances rather than waiting until I have dug beneath the surface; it goes back to the cultural shock of arriving in a new city. Why I judge humans so readily is because, essentially, I am antisocial.

My negative first impression of San Francisco resulted from my map being upside down. An erroneous left turn forced me to do a lap of a block (near Union Square) which the guidebooks tell you to avoid at all costs. It was filthy and teeming with homeless people, the pavement obscured by litter and spread-eagled bodies. I retreated back into my hotel, reassessed my route, and readied myself to venture out again.

With the map the correct way up, San Francisco revealed itself to be a much more agreeable city. I found the stop for the trams and permitted myself to be whisked up the street. I was immediately thankful as I had no idea San Francisco was built around 43 hills, my life-long avoidance of American films having left me ignorant of classic car chases. It occurred to me only then that the other cities I had visited, with the exception of Boston, had been bulldozer flat, and that Washington's Capitol Hill is not much more than a mole hill.

I alighted at the seafront and set off for the Golden Gate Bridge. It was an enjoyable three or four-hour amble to the bridge, across and back again - just what I needed to stretch my legs and blow away the cobwebs after three days on a train.

The walk beside the bay took me through beaches, marinas and protected bushland and repaid me with shifting perspectives of the bridge and the prison island of Alcatraz. I felt very safe. There were dog walkers, runners and cyclists making the most of the glorious weather. San Francisco can often be foggy and overrun with visitors, but I struck lucky again with just the occasional wisp of cloud breaking an otherwise clear blue sky, and it seemed as though there were no other tourists in town.

The suspension bridge, which opened in 1937, is a great feat of engineering and a much-loved icon of San Francisco, but would it be so adored if it were painted grey? As I meandered along, I found myself pondering the world's unloved bridges and what a coat of pink or yellow paint could do for them. To my uninformed eye, the Humber Bridge in the UK looks just like the Golden Gate Bridge, and yet my mother had hated the postcards of it we sent her every summer as children. Would she have been more appreciative if they had painted the Humber Bridge a snazzy colour?

It was blustery up on the Golden Gate Bridge and vehicles thundered alongside me, belching out their warm fumes. But the panorama of the bay and the metropolis crawling over distant hills more than compensated. A pod of dolphins frolicked below, piercing the water's surface with peals of pleasure.

There were several signs displaying helpline numbers for the Samaritans, and it saddened me to think how some people stand in the most picturesque of settings and only see despair. I have experienced my fair share of heartache and loss, but even in the darkest of times, I could always see the beauty in the world around me and the blessings in my life. That has been my saving grace. I am one of the lucky ones.

I am not sure how I envisaged San Francisco. Maybe with glittering tower blocks dominating the skyline and, of course, a great big orange bridge, what I didn't expect was the atmosphere of an English seaside town. Returning from the Golden Gate, I made my way down to Fisherman's Wharf; with the seagulls swooping noisily overhead and the shrieks of excitement coming from the amusement games, I was reminded of Skegness or Scarborough back home. It had a cheesy holiday vibe: more kiss-me-quick hat than California chic.

I idled away the afternoon on the piers before spending the evening knocking back beers with a former CIA officer I chanced upon. He used to be stationed in the Middle East and was well acquainted with the magazine I edited back in Dubai. To get him talking, I threw out some irresistible bait and asked: 'So how would you solve a problem like ISIS?'

This is a little trick of mine. Over the years, I have noticed if you get a middle-aged man pontificating on a subject he feels expert in, he will pay for your drinks to ensure you stay and listen. All you have to do is nod in agreement and turn controversial if the conversation looks like it is about to dry up. I am thus possibly the only person in the world to have enjoyed a free night on the booze thanks to Islamic State.

On my second day in the city, and with the map the right way up, I navigated a downhill route to the bay that took me through San Francisco's Chinatown, the oldest and largest in America. Chinese workers began migrating to California during the Gold Rush in the late 1840s, their numbers reaching about 12,000 by 1850. Denied landownership rights and mining claims, many gave up prospecting in favour of low-paid manual labouring jobs. They built roads, bridges and storage areas for the emerging wine industry and, most significantly, worked on the first transcontinental railway.

The reward for their productivity and contribution to opening up the west was a 10-year ban imposed in 1882 on new migrant workers arriving from China. The Chinese Exclusion Act, which aimed to halt rising unemployment and falling wages, was subsequently extended and only repealed in 1943. In a clear exercise in social engineering, Congress passed a blanket ban on all immigration from Asia in 1924, while simultaneously increasing permitted quotas for arrivals from western Europe. It seems Lady Liberty was actually rather selective about which tired, poor and huddled masses she wished to welcome. Limits were also put on migration from southern and eastern Europe.

I had not chosen the most evocative hour to explore Chinatown. Being shortly after nine in the morning, it was too early to suck on a deep-fried chicken foot or to see crowds gather around intense mahjong competitions. But there were enough elderly Chinese men, perched on tiny stools, watching the world go by, to get a sense of the place. I tried to imagine the tight alleyways when they housed brothels and opium dens and sheltered Chinese revolutionaries.

In 1906, San Francisco was struck by a 7.9-magnitude earthquake, triggering fires which destroyed 80 per cent of the city. The flames swept through the overcrowded Chinatown, erasing the ramshackle wooden buildings and tenement blocks, long considered an eyesore by the authorities. Afterwards, the area was rebuilt in the more attractive, tourist-friendly style seen today. I wandered around deliberating the merits and demerits of gentrification: how on the one hand, it suppresses the character that makes somewhere unique, while on the other, it makes the place safer and accessible for all.

The number one tourist attraction in San Francisco is the prison island of Alcatraz, which is considerably more accessible and safer than it used to be. The giant rock, whose name comes from the Spanish word for gannet, was the site of the first lighthouse on the west coast of the US. It later served as a harbour defence post and a military prison, before gaining notoriety as a maximum security prison, when it housed America's most dangerous criminals between 1934 and 1963.

The most famous resident was Al Capone, who was transferred to Alcatraz after reports surfaced of him receiving preferential treatment from prison guards elsewhere. His was a short stay, however. He was released early in 1939, deemed no longer fit for incarceration due to untreated syphilis ravaging his body. At the time of his death eight years later, it is said he had the mental age of a 12-year-old.

Capone, a husband and father, head of the most profitable crime syndicate in Prohibition America, survived countless attempts on his life only to be sent to his grave at the age of 48 by an STD. Had the women of yesteryear fully understood man's feebleness before lust, we would never have been written off as the weaker sex.

At Alcatraz, I witnessed once again how much Americans love an audio guide. They tend to shuffle around museums and sites of historical interest in slow-moving packs, shepherded along by a narrator and shouting comments to their companions at regular intervals: the volume on their headphones far higher than needed. Later, on my organised tour of the Napa and Sonoma wine regions, I realised why audio guides are so popular when I was subjected to seven hours of mindless ramblings by a man who thought he knew everything about anything. What I would have given for a skip button then.

Taxi drivers are instinctive tour guides. Wherever I go in the world, I always make a point of pumping them for information to extract additional value from my fare. The San Francisco taxi drivers were much more garrulous than their grunting counterparts in New York. They told me the city had lost its soul, the cost of living was soaring, and crime was on the increase.

Their views were echoed by an elderly lady who took me to a little-known vantage point after I asked her for directions. She was ancient, but flew up the hills, leaving me scurrying behind, panting.

'San Francisco used to be a village with painters, writers, dancers and poets until Silicon Valley moved in,' she said wistfully, as we gazed out over the houses towards the Golden Gate Bridge, partially hidden that day by low-hanging clouds. Skyscrapers clustered together in the distance on our right.

Similar sentiments were probably voiced during the Gold Rush in 1849, when hundreds of thousands of people flooded California from all over the world following James Marshall's serendipitous find. The population of San Francisco leapt from 850 to 25,000 in less than two years.

The Americans call it providence that within days of Marshall's gold discovery, and before the news was made public, the US signed a peace treaty with Mexico, giving it ownership of California and vast swathes of other land. The Gold Rush would set America on course to become the West's biggest economy, while bequeathing to the world the Levi jeans fashion label. By contrast, San Francisco's current population explosion has set back human intelligence through the engineering of a global smartphone addiction.

My final day in San Francisco was spent ticking off its other main parts: the financial district; the gay Castro area; and Haight-Ashbury, where the hippy movement was born. After a quick nose around the orderly and modern financial district, I took a bus to Castro, taking care to avoid walking through the civic centre, where, the taxi drivers warned me, violent and petty crime is rife.

It was probably not the best idea to try to get a feel of the gay area at eleven o'clock in the morning. Castro was mostly deserted, except for a few men treating their hangovers in café bars. The streets were colourful thanks to the rainbow flag pedestrian crossings and loud murals, but even at this early hour there was an intimidating maleness about the place. Sex was very much in your face (pun intended), with shops and restaurants boasting names such as Hand Job, Knobs, and Sausage Factory. I felt like a fish out of water.

Another bus took me on to Haight-Ashbury, where I hoped to catch a glimpse of a bygone era and not bump into Mr Crossover Toes, who had said it was his favourite place to hang out in San Francisco. A black woman and a long-haired relic of the 1967 Summer of Love fell into a discussion on the bus about how the neighbourhood had changed. It quickly turned into a heated debate about who had the greater right to live there. The conversation ended with the spat-out words 'I didn't ask you to start talking to me,' which met with the response 'Act your age, not your skin colour.'

It is fair to say Haight-Ashbury has had its day. There is an unnerving feel to the area, despite the best efforts of shopkeepers and bar owners to preserve a hippy appeal. Shifty-looking characters desperate to either buy or sell a fix have taken the place of the 'gentle people with flowers in their hair'.

I explored the streets extending out from the crossroads where a large clock permanently says twenty past four. According to modern folklore, this is when you should have your first hit of the day; I took it as forewarning of a potential crime spree as the hallowed time drew closer. The pavements were lined with smoke shops, tattoo and piercing parlours, and second-hand clothing and record stores - in my opinion, the word vintage is best reserved for Queen Victoria's silk bodices and cheddar cheese; the walls were covered with murals of Jimi Hendrix and Janis Joplin, as well as the obligatory graffiti feigning as art sprayed around by all countercultures.

I strolled the full length of the main road and my discomfort increased proportionately as it grew less and less salubrious. At the far end was a drug rehabilitation centre. Half a dozen or so people loitered outside waiting for their chance to enter, their bodies buckled by addiction.

Day was fast becoming dusk, so I didn't linger and instead retraced my steps to one of the bars I had passed earlier. As I sat enjoying a beer, there was a commotion outside. Blue flashing lights signalled the arrival of an ambulance and a young lad, who had collapsed on the street, was loaded up and whisked away. I had seen enough. It was a sad testament to an area trying to cling onto its romanticised past.

In today's multibillion-dollar global drug industry, there is no love, idealism or hippy revolution involved, and one hit can put you on the floor, or in a box.

I recovered my mood by paying yet another visit to the sea lions that have inhabited the docks at Pier 39 on San Francisco's waterfront for the past 25 years. The spectacle of dozens of sea lions coughing and farting on what should be some of the world's most expensive boat moorings filled me again with cheer.

TRAIN 5 - SAN FRANCISCO TO LOS ANGELES

I CONSIDERED TAKING the Greyhound bus to Los Angeles once I discovered that the journey from San Francisco would use up three precious segments on my US rail pass. At just $40, tickets were a bargain, but as with the $10 Chinese-run buses connecting New York with Boston, the internet is full of horror stories and warnings not to use them.

The Los Angeles Greyhound station gets particularly bad press as it is located in an isolated industrial area: the Lonely Planet guidebook describes it as unsavoury and to be avoided at all costs after dark.

So I decided to stick with the train, which had served me well thus far, and to avoid the hit on my rail pass, I shelled out the $71 fare. It immediately became clear why most tourists opt for the 90-minute plane ride.

The so-called train journey between San Francisco and Los Angeles - two of the most visited cities in America - involves a bus, a train and another bus, and takes more than half a day.

After the exhilaration of the *California Zephyr*, this section was a shock. The scenery was mostly agricultural land, but it was nothing like our countryside in the UK, with cows and sheep chewing on green pastures, hay bales drying in the sun, Mr Farmer bouncing along on his tractor, waving to ramblers walking along public footpaths, while his ruddy-cheeked wife sells free-range eggs at the farm gate. (Not to mention, the occasional controversial rows of polytunnels to force out-of-season fruit.)

There was no beauty to this landscape, no trees or hedge rows demarcating boundaries, no quaint farmhouses breaking up the scene. There were just mammoth spreaders sweeping over fields that stretched to the horizon. It was all about scale. Fields of mass production, lines of sheds crammed with animals, giant silos towering over the railway tracks. This was industrialised agriculture.

The soil was not rich, but dusty. There were no birds or bees. The flatness of the land accentuated the sense of desolation. Witnessing the enormous fields and the absence of nature's chaos, I understood why cheap food has no taste. I was left aghast by what I saw. It all felt so wrong.

As we drew close to Los Angeles, we caught sight of another important industry: a forest of nodding donkeys appeared out of nowhere, the ground around them dark with oil residue.

California is the fourth-largest oil-producing state in the US, and its hydrocarbons earnings, together with contributions from financial services, Silicon Valley, agriculture, the entertainment industry and other major sectors, help make the Golden State the world's fifth-biggest economy, ahead of India and the UK. Or at least they would, if it were a sovereign nation.

Again, I was shocked to see how big business was freely and visibly destroying the landscape in pursuit of profit. I couldn't understand how people accepted their country being abused in this way. Surely, it didn't have to be so raw...so uncompromising?

LOS ANGELES

SOME 13 HOURS after setting out from San Francisco, we arrived in Los Angeles. I had booked into a hotel one block away from Hollywood Boulevard. An alien concept before, I now understood what a block was. Marilyn Monroe and James Dean had supposedly stayed in this hotel, but that wasn't my reason for choosing it. The room was a bargain at only $100 a night, the cheapest of my trip so far. But I soon discovered the low price reflected the demise of the Hollywood area of Los Angeles.

Art Deco buildings, once symbols of 1920s grandeur, stand shabby and forlorn. Even the Walk of Fame has lost its lustre, the paving slabs cracking around long-forgotten stars. As a lone female, I felt uneasy walking down Hollywood Boulevard after dusk. In a rare burst of energy, I found myself almost running past the long stretches of shuttered shops, only relaxing once I reached somewhere that still had economic activity and the presence of others to comfort me.

There were plenty of people clustered around Donald Trump's star. They were taking turns to stamp on it, quite a contrast to the queues I had witnessed for his book signing in New York. By now, he was the frontrunner in the race to become the Republican presidential nominee. The Walk of Fame stars are bought and not bestowed, which explains the many obscure and unworthy names present (see strong example above) and the glaring omissions. The going rate in 2020 is $50,000.

Equally befitting America's consumerist soul, the iconic Hollywood sign, which keeps watch over the valley, began life as an advert for a property development. In a major triumph for the marketing department of Hollywoodland, it still stands almost a century later, minus the four final letters, and restored thanks to donations from Hugh Hefner, Alice Cooper and other upstanding members of the community.

Los Angeles is a poor city with pockets of riches, or maybe it's vice versa. Either way, it is strung out, with pleasant areas quickly giving way to grinding poverty and urban decay. The city is not conducive to walking and my early attempts to navigate by foot led me down some dodgy streets that made my pulse quicken. So I did something I rarely do and signed up for a hop-on hop-off bus tour.

I travelled to the end of the route and explored my way back. First up was Marina del Rey, which prior to Dubai's construction boom was the world's largest man-made marina - an agreeable development without much to delay a time-pressed tourist. Next, I abruptly stepped out of tranquillity into the mayhem of Venice Beach.

A lack of research left me unprepared for the sights, sounds and, most significantly, the smells that confronted me. The area is a magnet for alternative types: folks with dreadlocks, piercings and tattoos, who always carry around them a putrid fog of weed. As one of the least radical people you could ever meet, I couldn't wait to get out of there. Even the palms trees looked grungy.

Elbowing my way through the crowds watching street performers, I was astonished to see signs for freak shows involving people and animals with congenital disorders. (The marketing blurb uses slightly different wording.) The freak shows and some creepy canals are all that remain of the Venice-themed beachside entertainment resort that opened here at the dawn of the 20th century, having been built by tobacco millionaire Abbot Kinney.

Entirely misjudging the intellect of his target audience, Kinney envisaged a place of sophistication, with theatres, galleries and auditoria that would produce America's own cultural renaissance. Alas, his Shakespeare plays and operas found no audience in southern California, but the sideshows featuring oddities such as the world's smallest woman, the miniature railway and the beach proved an irresistible draw. And so the Venice of America became a carnival town, with fairground rides, dance halls, beauty pageants and freaks a plenty, and people flocked in from all around.

Its success was short-lived. Kinney died in 1920, and faced with rising competition from other resorts and falling revenues due to Prohibition, the town could not withstand the push of progress. In 1929, many of its canals were paved over to accommodate the motor car. That same year, just as the Great Depression took hold, oil was discovered in Venice. Within three years, nearly 350 wells were pumping out black gold; the derricks were everywhere, on the beach and in people's backyards, polluting the air and the pristine sand. As America's impoverished families stayed away, Venice fell into seedy neglect, eventually earning the label 'the slum by the sea'.

Laid-back Santa Monica, with its manicured public gardens and seafront promenade, was much more my cup of tea and, in hindsight, I should have made my base there. I lingered over some adult beverages on the breezy, café-lined Ocean Avenue before remembering I was meant to be hopping on and off a bus.

I headed for the centre of Los Angeles where I found myself wondering what Ped Xing had done to merit having a major road named after him. It was only after I noticed the sign appearing everywhere that I realised it was not honouring a Chinese man, but indicating a pedestrian crossing.

Downtown Los Angeles is described as up and coming. Its fabulous Art Deco structures are being brought back to life after decades of abandonment, and hip new bars and restaurants are popping up overnight. But there remained an emptiness that made me wary. It would need to up and come a lot further before I did a full exploration on foot.

We passed an area entirely taken over by tents, and from the upper deck, I could see there were no tourists in El Pueblo, the historical centre of Los Angeles; there were only traders and people down on their luck, surrounded by their possessions in plastic bags. I would later learn that as well as ranking among the 10 wealthiest cities in the world, LA is the homeless capital of America, with an estimated 55,000 rough sleepers. This is more than 10 times the total number of homeless people in England.

Even considering that the US has a far larger population than the UK - 320 million compared with 65 million - it is a staggering amount of people living without a roof over their head in just one metropolitan area. What makes it all the more inconceivable is that this is going on right under the noses of some of the most affluent people in the world, many of whom claim to have a social conscience.

I took pleasure in wandering around Beverly Hills wearing crumpled clothing and walking boots. Like Santa Monica, Beverly Hills is classed as a city in its own right, despite measuring less than eight square miles. On the diminutive Rodeo Drive, where celebrities go to be seen on private shopping sprees rather than ordering online, I stopped occasionally to press my sweaty nose against the display windows, hoping in vain for a *Pretty Woman* moment. By that, I mean I wanted to be shooed away like vermin, not mistaken for a prostitute and swept away to live a life of servitude as a sex slave for Richard Gere.

After briefly inspecting the towering hedges and bulletproof gates in the local housing estate, I took a breather in Our Lady of the Cadillac, as the church in Beverly Hills is irreverently known. It is where Frank Sinatra, Alfred Hitchcock and Rita Hayworth had their funerals, and Elizabeth Taylor began her husband collection.

Today, the big names of Hollywood are more likely to be adherents of Scientology, the cult or religion, depending on whom you believe, founded in 1954 by L. Ron Hubbard, a science fiction writer. There is nothing in that job description to rouse suspicion.

After finishing my bus tour, I nipped into a Scientology centre on Hollywood Boulevard expecting a Jehovah's Witness-style conversion attempt. I assume I was too poorly dressed to bother tapping up, given the well-heeled pickings elsewhere in the city; feeling ignored, I helped myself to a free DVD and left.

Since then, I have read all about Scientology's venerated galactic warlord, Xenu, and I realise I had a lucky escape, potentially saving hundreds of thousands of dollars in the process. It started me thinking about why the US seems more predisposed to cults and sects than the UK. That the first settlers of America were mostly religious zealots no doubt plays a part, but I also believe it is down to our superior television scheduling. This keeps impressionable minds occupied with a continuous diet of soap operas, dramas and not-infrequent documentaries mocking American cult devotees, while also positively encouraging heathen behaviour through trashy programmes such as *Love Island* and *Strictly Come Dancing*.

I did have an epiphany of sorts in Los Angeles, and it concerned beer. Beer drinkers must be prepared for frequent disappointment in the United States. The country's addiction to bottled Budweiser has long been ridiculed, but once you taste their draft lagers, which are always served devoid of bubbles, you might consider it the safest option.

One evening, while taking time out from trying to fathom the rules of American football, I challenged a bar man about the flatness of the beer he was selling. After some consideration, he gave his defence: 'Well, the beer travels a long way through pipes from the back of the bar.'

'Ah,' I replied. 'Now that I understand the logistical challenges you face, I am happy to pay for your bad beer.' I didn't say that, of course, as he seemed like a man who wouldn't understand sarcasm.

Another issue I had with the draft beer was the measurements. The bars measure beer in American fluid ounces, which means a

US pint is considerably smaller than the UK standard, at 16oz or 473ml, versus our 20oz or 568ml, and yet the prices are on a par. Not only does the smaller glass sit uncomfortably in the hand, the missing 4oz or 93ml means your thirst goes unquenched.

There are actually no regulations governing beer glass sizes in America and this encourages all kinds of mayhem. Servings are offered as small as 8oz and as big as 22oz, but more commonly as 10oz or 12oz. All draft beers come with laughably large frothy heads, yet never any bubbles.

After more disappointment than I was able to bear, I converted to bottled beers, which were joyously well-carbonated, and a Blue Moon accompanied by a slice of orange become my favourite, ahead of a Samuel Adams. But even then, the chaos continued, with bottles regularly being replaced, without warning, by an inferior tin can.

It was in the bars that my eyes were opened to the mindlessness of America's tipping culture. Here is how it works: a customer walks up to the bar and orders a bottle of beer; the bar tender takes one from the fridge, removes the lid, hands it over and receives payment; the customer blithely leaves a dollar tip. How is this a situation deserving a tip? Unless the customer had gone behind the bar and helped themselves to a beer, there was no other way to get the drink. With self-service not an option, the bar person has merely done their job, nothing more.

But it is in restaurants where tipping really gets out of hand. To spare you the mental arithmetic, the bill often comes with immense gratuities already calculated, with the options of leaving 17, 20 or 30 per cent extra. I would have to receive and accept a marriage proposal to merit giving a tip of 30 per cent. The standard everywhere else in the world is 10 per cent, and even that irks me. I don't get patted on the back at the end of a day's work and slipped some money; my salary is my recompense. If the restaurant staff need more money, the owners should raise the prices and pay them a higher wage.

Nothing ruins a meal out with friends quite like the tip conversation. I have come to the conclusion there is a masonic conspiracy among former serving staff that means it is incumbent upon them to coerce friends into giving tips - even when a service charge has already been included in the bill.

A gratuity should be given to reward excellent service, where someone has gone above and beyond what is expected to ensure you have a pleasant experience. But the tip mafia force you to leave a stack of notes and coins even when the service has been bad. It is as though their purpose in life is to extract money for the downtrodden of the hospitality industry, for whom they are willing to sacrifice decade-long friendships.

For me, a tip is a carefully weighed judgement that reflects the quality of service received. For the tip mafia, it is a public display of your inherent miserliness or generosity, and bears no relation to the experience had in the restaurant.

I developed two tactics to deal with tipping while in America. In restaurants that gave a free jug of water, I offset the expense of the tip by not ordering a drink.

If that was not an option, I would pay with as big a note as possible. This ensures the change is returned, allowing you to decide for yourself the size of tip you want to leave. It takes a lot of lip biting though, as the servers automatically ask whether you want the change regardless of how much you have given them. When you have left $100 for a $23 meal, it can be hard not to reply, 'Of course, I do. I'm not a bloody philanthropist.'

TRAIN 6 - LOS ANGELES TO SAN ANTONIO

IT WAS TEN at night when the *Texas Eagle* left Los Angeles. Travelling in the dark is the ultimate missed opportunity and all I saw of note until daybreak was a sprawling wind farm outside Palm Springs. In the interim, I had to contend with Doug from Yuma chewing my ear.

He gave me a detailed history of the US in relation to Yuma, a place I never knew existed. Whenever he mentioned another city, he felt the need to inform me how many miles it was from Yuma. This was rather wasted on me because aside from the fact I had no idea where Yuma was on a map, I am a girl and we are genetically incapable of visualising distances.

Curiosity has since got the better of me though, and I must tell you Yuma is hugely important as it supplies 90 per cent of America's lettuces during the winter months. Where would the great American burger be, during the winter months, without its limp green leaf from Yuma? Now that would have made an edifying train conversation, Doug.

It was the fourth week in November and the day before Thanksgiving. Most of my train companions were in good spirits, travelling to spend time with their families and feast on a dinner of roast turkey, ostensibly to give thanks for a good harvest, but in practice to give thanks for a successful trip to Walmart.

The tradition of Thanksgiving dates back nearly 400 years to September 1620, when a group of settlers and religious exiles set sail from England in the wooden galleon the *Mayflower* to start a new life in America, as the founders of Jamestown had done before them and thousands of New England Puritans would do after them.

The punishing two-month-long voyage put them at risk of starvation, disease and shipwreck, and life was just as gruelling once they arrived in the wilderness of the New World. Of the 102 men, women and children who began the journey, just 53 made it through the first harsh winter at Plymouth in present-day Massachusetts. At the end of the summer in 1621, the Pilgrim Fathers, as they are now known, celebrated their bountiful harvest with a three-day feast and gave thanks for being alive. It was attended by 90 Native Americans who had given them food and taught them how to work the barren land, thus ensuring their survival. In years to come, the indigenous population would be further rewarded with disease and violence.

According to official statistics, Americans like to spend the day after Thanksgiving, known as Black Friday, purchasing guns. Whereas in the UK, we tend to buy discounted sofas and kitchens in the sales to improve our home environment, or we might snap up some slightly imperfect, bargain-priced clothes, in the US, Black Friday consistently sets new records for the most guns sold in a single day. This is probably the consequence of having spent the previous 24 hours trying to get along with extended family.

I will never understand America's fixation with the right to bear arms in their Bill of Rights. The Second Amendment to the Constitution was written in 1791, when the world was a very different place. There would have been genuine concern among the 13 original colonies that formed the United States about potential threats to their right to exist as independent states which necessitated a 'well-regulated militia'. All white men, aged between

18 and 45, were armed and on standby to repel invasions, suppress insurrections and help enforce the law. They also acted as a check to the fledgling national government as the states feared tyrannical leadership above all else.

I believe there is no need for a citizen militia in 21st century America. The country has the world's best-equipped military and professional law enforcement agencies, as well as all the institutions needed to uphold democracy. And yet, there are an estimated 270 million privately owned guns in the US.

The type of weapons that can be bought over the counter today were inconceivable when the founding fathers put quill to parchment 200 years ago. In place of wooden, single-shot muskets, legal gun owners proudly polish assault rifles, capable of mass destruction in seconds. Why stop at guns? Surely a modern militia should have some tanks, surface-to-air missiles and weaponised drones? Maybe even a nuclear warhead? These too are arms that didn't exist in the 18th century. And what arguments can there be against resolving a neighbourly dispute with a harmless bit of waterboarding?

I find it absurd that school massacre after school massacre the authorities refuse to join the dots and repeal the Second Amendment. Gun advocates say it is their personal right to own a deadly weapon. But what of the right to life of the thousands of people shot dead every year? The Constitution is not inviolable - the human rights of slaves were long ignored, and Prohibition was written into the Constitution and then removed. The needless bloodshed could easily be stopped if only politicians would have the courage to stand up to the gun lobby and the National Rifle Association. Money should never be prioritised over human life.

I am proud to come from a country where the police are generally unarmed, and the passion some Americans show for having guns in the home is simply beyond my comprehension. I have seen women on TV enthusing over a semi-automatic weapon like it was a new pair of shoes. It ends lives, it is destructive, it cannot possibly be considered beautiful. Not even if it is decorated with lace, pretty flowers and butterflies.

I wonder what goes through people's minds: 'I am off to the supermarket, mustn't forget my gun.' Why? What's going to happen? Maybe a legal gun owner will go on a rampage after getting text dumped by his girlfriend?

Calls for tougher licensing laws usually follow a mass shooting, but licensing does not work. Mental illness is not a permanent state of being. It can manifest at any time once the pressure becomes too much. I found it unnerving to think I could be near people with guns in their possession. For me, as British girl, concealed carry just means hiding a tampon in your pocket on the way to the toilet.

We were in Arizona when dawn broke, revealing a parched, sandy terrain with scrubby bushes and dried-up river beds, set against a distant mountain backdrop. The colours grew vivid as the morning sun strengthened; later, dark clouds gathered to throw shadows over the uninhabited desert canvas.

For most of the day, we travelled through a vast emptiness, a beautiful nothingness. Everything was as nature intended, far removed from the agricultural devastation of the previous leg of my journey.

Small canyons rolled into and out of view as we ploughed across the rugged landscape. At one point, an enormous mudflat filled the windows. It was as if someone had mixed up the slide show, for it disappeared as quickly as it came.

The highlight of the journey occurred that afternoon when we drew alongside the Mexican border and I was able to gaze upon on the infamous Ciudad Juarez, one of the deadliest cities in the world. The contrast in wealth and development was stark. Youngsters grouped by the barbed-wire fence to wave at the passing train; they were so close that our eyes fleetingly met. Further on, gaping holes bore testimony to hopes for a better life.

The train stopped for a while in El Paso, and we all tumbled out for a leg stretch and a breath of Texan air. I stifled a squeal of delight as I clocked my first cowboy; well, a grey-haired man in a Stetson and pointy boots, to me that counts.

From El Paso, we crossed the Rio Grande and sped on towards my destination, San Antonio. At about nine o'clock at night, excited chatter broke out among a group at the end of my carriage. I went off to investigate and was told we were about to be treated to a paranormal phenomenon.

A mature gentlemen, who seemed of sound mind, explained that if we looked out into the night through the window on the right we might be lucky enough to see the famous Marfa lights: mysterious white orbs that flicker on and off and dart around. No one can say for sure what they are, he added.

We pressed our noses against the window and waited with bated breath until the mature gentlemen, who seemed of sound mind, urged: 'There! Look over there!'

Wonders do sometimes cease. I can say with 100 per cent certainty they were car headlights on a winding road. Mystery solved. It was classic American 'baloney'; we would never entertain such nonsense back home.

Marfa's headlamps had provided a service though, breaking the monotony of the dark hours on the train with some much-needed excitement. As I drifted in and out of sleep for the remainder of the journey, I kept chuckling about the paranormal phenomenon.

Finally, at ten to five in the morning, more than 30 hours after leaving Los Angeles, the *Texas Eagle* deposited me in San Antonio. My fellow travellers were quickly whisked away by bleary-eyed family members, and I was left in a car park devoid of taxis.

Much to my surprise, given the ungodly hour and the fact it was Thanksgiving, the ticket office was open. The jovial stationmaster booked me a taxi, while I helped myself to a free coffee. American customer service at its finest.

SAN ANTONIO

A PRE-DAWN ARRIVAL is the last thing any traveller wants in a country with ridiculously late check-in times. So I devised a cunning plan and booked a room with a top international hotel chain, paying rather more than I had been for other establishments. I was certain that in this era of online reviews they wouldn't turn me out onto the street, and at the very least, would let me snooze in their spacious reception area.

I also figured that to avoid the prospect of me dribbling on their soft furnishings and alarming other customers with my snoring, which I am told is indistinguishable from the growls of an angry bear, they would give me a room if one was available. Being Thanksgiving, it was a gamble, but the gamble paid off. By twenty past five, I was tucked up in a technically free, five-star bed, feeling smug and comfortable after another long train journey.

My motivation for visiting the Texan city of San Antonio was perhaps unusual. I had spotted it on the map just a few inches away from New Orleans and after consulting the highlights section of my guidebook, I learnt it was the home of the Alamo. I wasn't sure what the Alamo was, but I knew Johnny Cash had told us not to forget about it in a song that was a childhood favourite of mine. So that was it, I had to go and find out.

In that haphazard way, I ended up learning about another crucial chapter in the evolution of America. It turns out the Alamo was originally a mission base, established in 1718 by Spanish colonists to convert the native population to Catholicism. The site was later used as a garrison, which would lead to its special place in history.

In 1821, Texas and the territory known as New Spain broke away from the Spanish Empire to form Mexico. In the years that followed, settlers began arriving from the United States (with their slaves), turning the population of Texas increasingly American, and as the Mexican authorities became more and more dictatorial, support swelled for Texas to go it alone. After months of armed skirmishes with Mexican troops, independence was eventually declared on 2 March 1836.

The siege of the Alamo is remembered as a courageous struggle against overwhelming odds during the Texas Revolution. Despite being vastly outnumbered, 146 Texians[7] held out in the garrison for 13 days. They were eventually overcome on 6 March, when 2,600 Mexican soldiers charged the Alamo. Within hours, all those inside were dead including the fabled politician and soldier Davy Crockett; 600 Mexicans also lost their lives in the encounter.

History tells that the rallying cry 'Remember the Alamo! Remember Goliad!' led the ill-trained Texian army, which included American volunteers fighting in return for land grants, to a surprise victory on 21 April in the decisive battle of San Jacinto. The Mexican president, Antonio López de Santa Anna was captured and forced to recognise Texas as an independent nation. That was what Johnny Cash was singing about. He allowed us to forget the Goliad Massacre, in which more than 300 Texians perished, as it didn't scan quite so well. Not much rhymes with massacre, if you think about it, other than brassica.

---

[7] Residents of Mexican Texas, and later the Texan Republic, were known as Texian.

The Republic of Texas lasted until 1845, when it was annexed to the United States at the behest of the settlers who wanted to see the country stretch right across to the Pacific Ocean. Texas became the 28th state in the federation, and America, imbued with the spirit of manifest destiny, showed itself ready to fight for further territorial expansion.

The 1846-48 Mexican-American War turned the US into the giant nation it is today, while Mexico halved in size, ceding California, Nevada, Utah, most of Arizona, and chunks of New Mexico, Colorado and Wyoming to its neighbour. The purchase of Alaska from Russia in 1867 for $7.2m would complete the jigsaw puzzle of continental America. (Florida was bought for $5m in 1821, ending some 250 years of mostly Spanish rule over the peninsula.)

Texas was independent for less than a decade, but you wouldn't think so from all the Lone Star flags fluttering proudly in San Antonio today. Texan first, American second is their motto. Their difference from the east coast is perceivable in everything: in the food, in the music and, most of all, in the people, who lack any affectation. They are as down-to-earth folk as you can find, and I was thankful they kept their guns hidden from my eyes.

America was initially hesitant to annex Texas as debate was raging in the country over slavery, and it was thought a large, slave-holding state entering the union would worsen the already volatile political atmosphere. Congress was also loath to take on the debt the republic had racked up in its short life. Texas joined anyway, but it was agreed it would retain its debts and the rights over its public land.

This would prove to be a costly decision. The federal government lost out on the opportunity to claim royalties from the oil, discovered half a century later, which would transform Texas into the US' biggest energy producer. At the start of 2020, Texas was pumping 5.4 million barrels of oil a day - half the entire output of Saudi Arabia. The state government takes 25 per cent of all hydrocarbons revenues and is so rich that it doesn't charge any personal income tax. This explains the happy-go-lucky nature of the Texan people, and why they have the confidence to walk around in cowboy regalia in the 21st century.

Quite by chance, I had chosen to visit San Antonio on the day that thousands of people turn out to witness the switching on of the Christmas lights and to cheer a festive float parade along the city's winding river.

The holiday season in the US continues from Thanksgiving until New Year's Day, and for a month and a half, Americans wish each other 'Happy Holidays' every time they part. Not only is this tiresomely repetitive, it is also three times longer than the total number of days' leave most working Americans get in an entire year.

The festive float parade was a washout. Torrential rain forced its abandonment after just 20 minutes, sending sodden Santas scurrying for shelter and leaving business owners wringing their hands over lost trade.

I took refuge in a bar with a couple from Louisiana. We discussed the coordinated terror attacks that had happened days earlier in Paris, wiping out 130 lives, including 90 concert goers. They defended US gun laws, saying if the assaults had happened in America some people would have 'been carrying' and could have ended it sooner.

The pair took me to Durty Nelly's, a legendary Irish bar in San Antonio, made famous by its raucous sing-alongs. The master of ceremonies, seated at an upright piano, was raking in the money as people tipped him generously, both to start and stop songs.

I left well acquainted with the *Aggie War Hymn*, the official song of Texas A & M University. The rousing tune, which opens with the words 'The eyes of Texas are upon you', was written by a soldier sat in a trench in France during World War I. Little did he know, he was changing the fortunes of buskers and bands back home forever. The song tugs on the wallet strings of every Texan and is therefore a favourite of live performers. It gets played so regularly you could set your watch by it.

There are no strangers at Durty Nelly's, only friends you haven't yet met, I was informed when I returned the next day and was joined at my table by a young lad, who herded cattle for a living. He and his parents gave me the first full-on hangover of my trip and I have no recollection of anything we discussed. Had I known then what I know now about the mass production of meat in America, the modern, baseball cap-wearing cowboy would have had his ears bashed all evening about the ethics of confinement farming and the use of hormones and antibiotics in the livestock industry.

TRAIN 7 - SAN ANTONIO TO NEW ORLEANS

TEXAS IS AMERICA's second-largest state after Alaska and nearly twice the size of Germany. I left knowing I had barely scratched the surface of what it had to offer - San Antonio doesn't have much other than the Alamo - and I vowed to return one day for a more thorough examination.

The *Sunset Limited* departed at twenty five past six in the morning. It was a dark, overcast day, so I allowed myself to nod off; I'd also had a bit of a heavy night with the unethical cowboy. The land was flat, and the scenery flitted between forest and field. Travelling eastwards, the trees once again displayed autumnal colours: golden yellows, burning reds and turdy browns.

I woke as we drew into Houston at eleven o'clock. The station was ugly, and beyond it, I could see huge flyovers pouring traffic into a city centre populated with skyscrapers. It was cold outside, and I noted how a lack of sunshine influences your mood and perceptions of a place.

We moved on through a grey industrial landscape of pipes and chimneys belching steam and who knows what else. At Beaumont-Port Arthur, an influx of passengers filled the train.

Someone started playing music from their phone. There was raucous laughter, and the southern drawl was clear to hear. We rolled across Lake Charles serenaded by BB King, the calm of the morning supplanted by commotion. I was excited about what lay in store in New Orleans.

It was almost ten at night when the train pulled into Union Station. Having read an obsessive amount about crime levels in the city, I decided to leave exploring for the following day and immersed myself instead in some American culture by seeing what was on the telly.

I was treated to an episode of *Kourtney & Kim Take New York* - my first ever Kardashian experience. It opened with a greasy haired guy adjusting his genitalia as he exited a hotel door, grossly overstating his endowment. His girlfriend admonished him, and the incident teed up 20 minutes of him being depicted as a slob and her (I never concluded whether it was Kourtney or Kim) the patronising, controlling girlfriend. He ends up going to see his therapist for expensive advice on how to deal with the incessant nagging. Fortunately, money is no object for him, and he is able to diffuse the situation by checking into another hotel room and scattering crisps and sweets all over his specifically requested king-sized bed.

It was painful viewing. The protagonists, if that is not too grand a word, were stupefyingly vacuous, prone to bouts of high drama which necessitated whingey voices and lots of phone calls on loudspeaker. In between, there were laughably sincere discussions about fashion and clothes shopping, like they were the most important things in the world.

It horrified me to think of all the impressionable viewers around the world being led to believe this is not only normal behaviour, but the lifestyle to which they should aspire. These youngsters are blind to the fact that fashion is just a means to extract money from people and the TV series itself part of a consumerist conspiracy to get those who can least afford to do so to waste all their money on designer goods, expensive make-up and plastic surgery. It would be ingenious if it wasn't so tragic.

The weather forecast that followed was much more entertaining. It was presented by an exuberant meteorologist who sounded, to my British ears, like an Italian-American mafioso. The overdramatised monologue in which the benevolent gangster recommended we wrap up warm and issued a caring weather alert for small vessels at sea, all while gesticulating wildly, left my mouth agape.

But the real gems of American television, I came to realise, are the adverts for prescription medicine. The commercials comprise about 30 seconds promoting the benefits of a drug, followed by two minutes of quick-fire warnings about why you should steer clear of the drug. Commonly cited side effects include loss of vision, internal bleeding, seizures and 'in rare cases, coma or death'. It makes a trip to the doctor's sound like a game of Russian roulette.

For the pharmaceutical industry, these advertisements have the equivalent of the Delia or Jamie Oliver effect on obscure foodstuffs. The idea of petitioning your doctor for a particular drug is anathema to Brits, who elevate their GPs to God-like status and trust in their superior knowledge. The adverts would have provoked some moral outrage in me were it not for my experience of profit-driven private healthcare in Dubai. My bathroom cabinet could keep a small African village stocked with medicine, which I never needed to be prescribed.

Medical adverts are relentless in America, and they leave you with a warped impression of the average marital home. There is the exhausted and depressed, yet beautifully made-up housewife unable to function without her Xanax. She is battling suicidal thoughts because she is kept awake all night by her handsome and successful husband who needs somewhere to put his five-hour erection, which he refuses to accept is a side effect of his Viagra medication and not a desired outcome. Happily, she can now sneeze with confidence thanks to her decision to start using Tena Lady, but he is gambling with an increased risk of heart failure.

NEW ORLEANS

IT WASN'T JAZZ that tempted me to New Orleans. I have hated jazz ever since I had the misfortune to go interrailing during the 1994 European Summer of Jazz festival. For an entire month, I was haunted by the soporific thumpity-thump of the double bass as every open space in every city in Europe was given over to a jazz ensemble. On the scale of annoyances, that summer, I rated jazz musicians one level above those scraggy-haired students who sit crossed-legged in public squares drumming.

I was in New Orleans for the food and architecture. The cuisine of Louisiana reflects the ethnic diversity of its people and a complicated colonial history. The southern melting pot, in the literal sense of the word, combines French, Spanish, African and Native American influences to give us Cajun and Creole stews - with their celery, onion and pepper bases - Po-boy sandwiches, sweet beignets, and alligator served in a hundred different ways, to list just a few of the gastronomic experiences on offer.

Creole was the name given to descendants of the region's European colonisers: the French, who originally settled Louisiana, naming the area after King Louis XIV of France, and the Spanish who followed them. Cajun was the Anglicised name given to French settlers expelled from the colony of Acadia in Canada by the British in the mid-18th century, many of whom eventually made their home in Louisiana.

The expulsions occurred during the North American prelude to the global Seven Years' War of 1756-63, which saw Britain emerge victorious and in possession of French-speaking Canada. The peace treaty also gave Britain the French lands east of the Mississippi River and allowed France to retain possession of New Orleans and its lands west of the Mississippi, prompting the influx of Cajuns to Louisiana.

It later emerged that France had secretly ceded Louisiana to Spain in a treaty inked in 1762, so Spain took control of New Orleans and the lands west of the Mississippi for the next 40 years, adding yet more flavours into the cooking pot.

Louisiana ended up in American hands by way of Napoleon. The diminutive Frenchman, fresh from seizing power and keen to re-establish France's empire, convinced Spain to hand back the territory in 1802. The Spanish agreed, believing that a French-held Louisiana would provide a buffer against the newly independent and ambitious United States, whose settlers were already spreading into their lands.

Less than a year later, after failing to put down a French Revolution-inspired slave rebellion in the Caribbean, Napoleon tore up his plans for North America and sold Louisiana to the US for $15m. In an instant, the young country doubled in size. It was the deal of the century.

The 1803 Louisiana Purchase saw America take control of 828,000 square miles of land, stretching from the Gulf of Mexico to Canada and from the Mississippi to the Rocky Mountains - some 40 per cent of the US today. The acquisition would open the continent to westward migration and put the US among the leading powers of the day.

Sometimes all it takes is a few plates of free food to access a closed off mind, and so it was that I found myself appreciating the rhythms of America's deep south in the Spotted Cat jazz bar on Frenchmen Street in New Orleans. In this gem of a place, every beer comes with a helping of jambalaya or gumbo. With my head pleasantly foggy from an undetermined number of (bottled) Blue Moons and my mouth tingling with spice, jazz didn't seem quite so terrible after all. The crooning of the gravel-voiced frontman and the melancholic strains of trumpet and trombone fitted the dingy surrounds, and on that wet November night, I made my peace with the double bass.

While the food alone would be enough to draw tourists to Nawlins, as the locals pronounce it, the star attraction is the charming architecture of the city's historic centre. The rows of quaint townhouses with gas lamps, shutters and wrought iron balconies seem so out of place in 21st century America that it feels as though you have stumbled onto a film set.

Although the area is known as the French Quarter, most of the buildings date from the period of Spanish rule. In 1788, 80 per cent of New Orleans was devastated by fire after a candle ignited an altar cloth in Chartres Street, and a second great conflagration followed in 1794. The Spanish rebuilt the city, replacing the wooden structures with brick buildings and adding the now characteristic balconies and courtyards.

The French Quarter is set out on a grid pattern: one half is residential, while the other is lined with boutique hotels, enticing restaurants and galleries that almost convince you to splurge on impractical pieces of artwork.

The quarter is serene until late morning when the tour buses disgorge their excitable, slow-moving cargo and scores of musicians descend with their unwieldly instruments to hustle for tips. Although New Orleans is the birthplace of jazz, the song that gets played the most by the city's many buskers is *Onward Christian Soldiers*. I am convinced they choose the most turgid piece of music ever composed so that a crowd of passing tourists will drop some coins in their box but won't stay to listen, and the band can stop playing.

Bourbon Street is an abomination in an otherwise beautiful district. The handsome colonial façades have been lost in the chaos of neon signs advertising the bars, souvenir shops and, in the loosest sense of the word, the gentlemen's clubs that line the street. The music that bowls down the road is the same uninspired, throbbing DJ beats heard the world over rather than the sounds for which the city is famed. Maybe it was the time of year, maybe it is what people seek on a night out, but to my nostrils Bourbon Street stank of a cocktail of wee, vomit and sewage.

The heart of old New Orleans is the bustling Jackson Square, where fortune tellers and artists gather with musicians to earn a living. The square is towered over by the white-washed St Louis Cathedral with its three soaring steeples, while a statue of General Andrew Jackson astride a bronze horse occupies the centre.

The general, who was of Irish stock, is revered for defeating the British in the 1815 Battle of New Orleans, which was the final and biggest battle in the War of 1812. (The Americans are still learning how history should be documented.)

The US' had instigated the war, its first foreign conflict since independence, in protest at Britain's blockade of France interrupting its trade with Europe and American sailors being pressganged into the Royal Navy.

In a cruel twist of fate, General Jackson's great victory was null and void as, unbeknown to the soldiers, a peace treaty ending the war had been signed two weeks before the Battle of New Orleans commenced. News travelled slowly in those days as the Scottish inventor Alexander Graham Bell had yet to be born and Samuel Morse still believed his gift to humanity involved portrait painting.

Along with America's failure to annex Canada, the abiding legacy of the War of 1812 is the poem a young lawyer from Baltimore wrote about it, entitled *The Defence of Fort M'Henry*. Set to the tune of a British drinking song and renamed *The Star Spangled Banner*, the United States would adopt it as their national anthem, more than a century later. While it is commonly known that the stars on the spangly banner represent the 50 states that make up America, it is less well known that the stripes represent the 13 original English colonies.

Oblivious to all this history, I had booked myself into the Andrew Jackson Hotel on Royal Street. It was under renovation and the receptionist apologised in advance for any disturbances.

She then proceeded to tell me the building used to be a boarding school and it is haunted by five boys who died in the great conflagration of 1794.

She said guests have reported hearing children giggling, being pushed out of bed, belongings disappearing and reappearing, and that most favourite poltergeist pastime - lights being switched on and off again. I was just pleased to learn the ghosts came at no extra charge and there was no need to tip them.

To make the most of my time in Louisiana, I signed up for a tour of a plantation museum and a swamp. Although the Spanish, British and French first introduced slaves to America, it was after independence that their numbers peaked. In 1790, there were 654,000 slaves registered in the south. By 1860, the figure had soared to 3.95 million. Slaves accounted for nearly half the population of the southern states, where they were forced to work on sugar, tobacco and cotton plantations. Slavery was not just the backbone of the south's economy: in the mid-1830s, cotton accounted for more than half of all exports from America.

The former sugar plantation at Oak Alley is said to be one of the best to visit, but I am not sure what criteria that claim is based on. It certainly isn't because it gives the most painstaking and accurate portrayal of the exploitation and suffering of slaves. The focus was entirely on the wealthy, land-owning family - the 50-minute detailed tour of the plantation house, complete with guides in period costume, did not take in the replica slave lodges due to 'insufficient time'.

In any case, the accommodation blocks leave you little wiser about the human cost of slavery. The information is limited, with just some shackles on display and a suggestion that one of the biggest privations for a slave was not being able to choose their own clothes. The estate owned 113 slaves in 1848: 20 ran the house and the others were deployed in the fields. Their names are listed, along with their purchase price, and a note to say this is all that remains of their history.

The swamp tour acquainted me with the official state reptile, the alligator. One third of Louisiana is wetland, which is the perfect habitat for gators, as the locals affectionately call them. We passed a sunny afternoon navigating the bayou (that's Cajun French for wetlands) in the noisiest of boats, cutting through the reflections of overhanging trees and generally disturbing the peace and tranquillity.

There were dozens of snoozing alligators to spot and others doing a fine job pretending to be logs. As an unadvertised bonus, we also saw turtles, herons and some chubby racoons. The obesity epidemic among the Louisiana racoon community can easily be explained by the handfuls of marshmallows our boatman was throwing at them.

He fed us dinner party-worthy alligator facts. The sex of a gator is determined by the temperature inside the eggs. When cold, their hearts beat once every seven minutes. On land, alligators can reach speeds of up to 35 miles an hour, but they tire quickly. I ended the day much more enlightened about alligators than slavery.

Excursions outside New Orleans help you to understand the unique topography of the area and the complex engineering that goes into protecting the city from flood waters. You get to see the pumping stations and drainage channels, the levees and flood walls, which tragically failed in 2005, as well as Lake Pontchartrain, the second-largest saltwater lake in the US, which lies to the north of the city.

New Orleans is surrounded by water, with Lake Borgne to the east, the Mississippi River to the south and beyond that, the Gulf of Mexico. Most of the city sits below sea level - about 6ft lower on average than the Gulf.

The high water table made for a less-than-restful afterlife for the city's earliest residents: their coffins would often float to the surface during the annual floods, posing a hazard to health and a surprise to dog walkers. When the original St Peter Street cemetery was closed due to overcrowding in the late 18th century, it was decided the new one would only accommodate tombs.

The coffins were placed in aboveground marble structures and the intense Louisiana heat accelerated decomposition to such an extent that after a year and a day just bones remained. This 'natural cremation' meant the vaults could be opened for use by other family members, with one tomb able to serve many generations. (In the unfortunate circumstance of several deaths in quick succession, temporary 'ovens' could be rented.) It was a solution to both the resurfacing coffin problem and the lack of cemetery space. The tombs grew more and more elaborate as the number of inhabitants increased, and the cemeteries are now a popular stop on the New Orleans tourist trail.

The cemetery tours are usually combined with a visit to the now infamous 9th Ward. As the city's poorest district, holidaymakers would have given it a wide berth prior to 2005, but it is where the destruction of Hurricane Katrina can still be seen. Dozens of homes remain abandoned - some boarded up, others open to the elements - and the spray-painted Xs, used by rescue teams to mark searched properties, have yet to fade away.

It was nearing the end of August when Katrina hit. Many of those living in the 9th Ward would have been waiting for their next welfare payout, stretching out their last dollars, unconcerned that their homes stood on land 4ft below sea level. In any case, most of the houses in the area were raised on stilts, the only way to get insurance following previous floods.

When the mandatory evacuation of New Orleans was ordered, an estimated 20 per cent of the city's residents had no money for a bus or train ticket or a hotel room. About 100,000 people didn't have their own means of transport and so they decided to stay put.

For 1,833 souls that would prove to be a fatal decision. For certain residents of the 9th Ward, it would mean a two-week wait to be rescued. Others would find themselves among the 20,000 people who took refuge in the Super Dome stadium, where they too became trapped. Some would join the looters that ransacked parts of the city as law and order broke down.

At the time, New Orleans was protected by 350 miles of levees, with 24 pumping stations acting as a second line of defence. The levees were built 13-18ft high, but it has since been acknowledged they were poorly maintained. On 29 August 2005, as Hurricane Katrina battered the coast, there was a storm surge 14-17ft high.

Some earthen levees were washed away, while others broke under the strain of trying to hold back the water, overwhelming the pumping stations. Flood water 12ft deep rushed into the city, submerging thousands of single-story homes in the 9th Ward and taking out telephone and electricity connections.

In the city alone, at least 200,000 homes were destroyed, while 80 per cent of the greater New Orleans area was covered in flood water. It would take 21 days to pump the water out of the city as the levees now trapped the flood water in. The damage to New Orleans was estimated at $108bn and the rescue effort would come under heavy criticism for being badly coordinated.

The French Quarter escaped the flooding unscathed and it was no fluke. When the city was established by the French in 1718, they sited it on the highest terrain on a crescent-shaped bend on the Mississippi River, leaving the surrounding swamp land for farming. As the population expanded in the centuries that followed, these low-lying, outer areas were gradually subsumed into the city with the help of drainage systems.

Since Hurricane Katrina, $20bn has been spent on bolstering New Orleans' flood defences. But scientists warn of worse disasters to come. The reclaimed swamp land is sinking. The levee system, which protects the city, prevents annual flooding and sedimentation, causing the land to sink by 1-5 centimetres each year. That doesn't sound worth losing sleep over, but calculated over a century, it amounts to a significant drop.

Beyond the flood defences, the wetlands are also vanishing. Climate change-driven sea level rise, coastal erosion, and damage from oil and gas extraction have caused dozens of barrier islands to fall under water. A quarter of the state's wetlands have disappeared since 1932, with some 2,000 square miles lost from Louisiana's coastline. Much of southern Louisiana will cease to exist unless coastal restoration projects can halt the sea's advance. Many small communities are under threat. It is quite probable that the New Orleans tourist trail of the future will boast Lost Louisiana boat tours as well as visits to the world's first diabetic racoon colony.

TRAINS 8 + 9 – NEW ORLEANS TO MIAMI

THE JOURNEY FROM New Orleans to Miami broke me. Most people in their right mind wouldn't even consider attempting it by train, particularly as it now entails going via Washington. (The direct service from Los Angeles to Orlando in Florida was put out of action by Hurricane Katrina and never resumed.) Determined to get around the US by rail, I had to commit nearly three days of my life to the journey.

There was no observation carriage on the train to Washington and I soon understood why. For hour after hour after hour, there was nothing to see except uninspiring woodland. I adore trees, but these were just bare branches whizzing past the window. Even the wooden houses, which had captured my interest four or five weeks earlier, no longer enthralled me. They had become bland features of the landscape, unchanging in shape and style as I moved from east to west and back again.

We left New Orleans at eight in the morning, about an hour behind schedule, and I snored through most of Mississippi. I woke when we stopped at Birmingham in Alabama. The platform was dilapidated and in need of weeding. A woman of advanced years joined the train for what was her first ever rail journey. Her neighbour showed her how to adjust the seat and pointed out the toilets. 'I won't be using that,' she announced to the carriage. 'I only have one kidney.' The neighbour's father had just died and was on the way to the funeral. The pair passed cathartic hours discussing hospices and cancer.

A black lady sat beside me. Our brief conversation revealed her astonishing knowledge of the bible and her equally astonishing ignorance of geography. When I told her I was from a village near London, she clarified, 'London, Paris?'

I found it mindboggling to think that not so long ago this woman could have been arrested, fined or even imprisoned for sitting next to me under America's racial segregation laws. In 1890, the Louisiana Separate Car Act was passed, preventing black passengers and 'people of colour' from travelling in the same train carriages as whites. They were even allocated separate toilets to use. It was one of scores of local and state laws that for nearly 100 years would enforce segregation in all aspects of daily life in the American south, including schools, colleges, hospitals, parks, prisons, churches, cemeteries, restaurants and bars.

This legalised discrimination was born out of fears of black advancement following the end of the Civil War. With the 13th amendment to the Constitution abolishing slavery and involuntary servitude in 1865, some 4 million people had been given their freedom. They now had the right to an education, to own property and to hold public office. The federal government established a bureau to provide for their immediate needs and many soon found jobs in public institutions.

This raised the hackles of the southern states. They had lost the war and their plantation economy was in ruins following the emancipation of the slaves. In an effort to re-establish a cheap labour force, local and state authorities began passing legislation restricting what African Americans could and couldn't do. Meanwhile, in Tennessee, a group of confederate veterans founded the Ku Klux Klan. The KKK terrorised the newly freed men and women, employing arson and murder to intimidate and exert control over them.

The north's outrage at the treatment of former slaves prompted further constitutional amendments. The 14th amendment (1868) granted citizenship to everyone born or naturalised in the United States and gave all people equal protection under the law. The 15th amendment (1870) stated no one could be denied the right to vote on account of race, colour, or previous condition of servitude.

But critically, the federal government decided not to institute a policy of land redistribution. It also established separate schools and hospitals for former slaves, thereby sowing the seeds of segregation.

When federal troops withdrew from the southern states after the period of reconstruction, the protection afforded to African Americans left with them. Black political and social mobility was halted in its tracks. Racial segregation and marginalisation entered the statute books as the plantation states moved to preserve their white-dominated society.

'White Only' signs became ubiquitous. Hanging over ticket booths, waiting rooms, toilets and drinking fountains, they provided a constant reminder that African Americans were to be considered second-class citizens. When the legality of segregation was challenged in the courts, the official line was the 'Jim Crow' laws, as they were crudely known[8], kept blacks separate but equal. In reality, the facilities allocated to them were inferior to those for whites and they were poorly maintained.

As the years passed, the laws proliferated and became more audacious. In some states, skin colour trumped safety, giving white motorists the right-of-way at junctions. In others, there were curfews and enforced sterilisations; white-only shops and entire towns off limits to blacks. In flagrant violation of the Constitution, African Americans were denied equal employment opportunities

---

[8] Jim Crow was a blackface character in a minstrel show that began touring in the 1830s.

and blocked from voting in elections. Interracial marriages were also forbidden.

Although there were no segregation laws beyond the southern border states, racial discrimination was endemic in the rest of the country too, particularly when it came to housing and jobs. Former slaves and their descendants headed in their thousands to cities in the north as mechanisation replaced manual labour in agriculture in the south. Affluent whites, now in possession of motor cars, moved into exclusive suburban developments, leaving inner-city ghettos to form. While new out-of-town shopping precincts thrived, city centres were left to decay and black urban poverty became rife.

The irony is that while African Americans were being denigrated and marginalised, millions of people from across the world were emigrating to the US, hailed as the land of freedom and opportunity.

It would only be in 1964, exactly 99 years after slavery was abolished, and following a decade-long campaign of civil disobedience, that the Civil Rights Act would outlaw racial discrimination in America. It would be another year before the Voting Rights Act was passed, echoing what had already been declared in the 15th amendment some 95 years earlier.

You have to ask why it was acceptable to ignore the constitutional amendments of 1865-70, but the clause concerning the right to bear arms is considered inviolable. Just as incomprehensible to me is the fact that segregation was allowed to continue after World War II, when American troops, including black conscripts, laid down their lives to stop fascism and Nazi Germany's attempt at creating a white master race.

Following the war, as bombed-out European nations focused on reconstruction, the US deftly manoeuvred to position itself as the leader of the free world, becoming host to the United Nations, the International Monetary Fund and the World Bank. Yet when the UN published its Universal Declaration of Human Rights in 1948, America itself was contravening the opening statement that 'All human beings are born free and equal in dignity and rights.'

My plan had been to scurry around a museum in Washington mid-way through the expedition to Miami, but we arrived the next day more than two hours behind schedule, leaving just time for a quick lunch in Union station.

The change in train didn't bring a change in scenery, and until we reached the Florida peninsula, there was little to draw my attention through the window. The entire journey was a waste of my life. I can't read on the move due to travel sickness, so I was sat for 55 hours mostly doing nothing.

About 15 hours were passed in the role of therapist for a chap in his seventies who insisted on telling me about his recent string of failed relationships 'with older women'. He was hard of hearing and failed to pick up on my not-so-subtle hints that I wasn't interested in his sordid sex life. I had to lean in close to his hairy ear whenever I felt obliged to comment.

It was early evening when we finally rolled into Miami, and I vowed it would be my last train ride for a very long time. Just the thought of taking a train back to New York to complete the circuit made me feel sick.

The final two segments on my precious rail pass could go in the bin.

MIAMI

I HAD BOOKED a hotel on Ocean Drive in the South Beach area of Miami without realising I would be arriving unwashed and dishevelled into one of the most happening streets in the US. I was mortified to have to drag my suitcase through a heaving bar to get to the hotel reception.

A scalding shower and a fresh pair of knickers helped restore my dignity before I ventured out to look at all the cool people. After nearly three days on a train, the loud music and exuberance was almost too much to bear. I had a tasty Cuban dinner at Gloria Estefan's restaurant - she cooks much better than she sings - then headed back to savour the luxury of having a bed.

The next morning brought news of a shooting and a stabbing in the neighbourhood. The shooting involved a bank robber being sent to an early grave by the police, while the stabbing occurred at an arts fair and was mistaken for performance art. Naturally, I set about exploring with an even more heightened sense of alert than usual, but it wasn't long before I relaxed into Miami's laidback ways.

Until the beginning of the 20th century, Miami Beach was a reptile-infested strip of land, comprising sand dunes, scrub and swamp. Development started in 1913, after some shrewd landowners decided the peninsula would make an ideal winter resort for wealthy northerners looking to escape the cold. A massive construction boom in the 1920s saw Art Deco hotels dot the landscape as America's tropical playground took shape. A hurricane caused widespread devastation in 1926, but the city quickly bounced back, and Miami still boasts more than 1,200 Art Deco structures today.

This spectacular architecture transports you back to the Roaring Twenties. As I strolled along the palm-lined boulevards, admiring the bold lines and rounded contours, the pastel blues, yellows, pinks and greens, I felt I ought to be wearing long, white gloves with a cigarette holder pinched between my stubby fingers.

Congress, Crescent, Betsy Ross, St Moritz…the buildings project their names with style. Giant umbrellas front the hotels, sheltering chattering drinkers and diners, and I wondered how many appreciated the beauty of the architecture around them.

Only when I crossed the back alleyways, with their collections of bins did I remember I was in a potentially dodgy area of America and could get mugged at any moment.

It was on the steps of his Miami mansion that the flamboyant fashion designer and man-about-town Giovanni Versace was gunned down in 1997. A taxi driver told me the city had never been the same after the murder. The stars sold up and left, and many of the bars and clubs closed their doors, ending a decade of unrestricted hedonism.

I didn't make it to downtown Miami and the Little Havana and Little Haiti districts beyond it. I was so enchanted by the architecture and walkability of the Miami Beach area, and the unexpected feeling of safety that I wasn't bothered about seeing what else the city had to offer. It was also Miami Art Week which meant the museums near my hotel were free.

The exhibition at the Frost Museum of Art included tourism posters from the 1930s. One in particular still captured the essence of Miami: 'We are blessed with a smiling climate - the air is charged with health and perfume. There is the lure of open sea and protected bay - and it is playland for everyone. This land of palms and sunshine with arms wide, welcomes you.'

At South Beach's convivial tourist information office, I signed up for a day trip to Key West. It was a four-hour bus ride each way - a mere blink of the eye compared to my monster train journeys – and it was well worth the early start.

The drive took us through the lush mangroves of the Everglades, across 42 bridges linking the string of islands known as the Florida Keys, and onwards to the southernmost point of continental America. The longest bridge stretches for nearly seven miles, the right side lapped by the Gulf of Mexico and the left by the Atlantic.

We followed the US 1 highway, which runs for nearly 2,400 miles up to the US/Canada border. Travelling in the opposition direction, it is the road to nowhere. A zero-mile sign marks its end in Key West.

The 113-mile section linking the Florida Keys is called the Overseas Highway and it is built on the remnants of a railway line that opened in 1912 and connected Key West with the mainland. In 1935, a hurricane destroyed the railway, washing away about 40 miles of track, and it was never repaired. The old station in Key West is now a small museum.

Key West is at turns a charming backwater, a tourist trap and a traveller's haven. It is where Harry S Truman[9] retreated to 11 times during his presidency, and I can see how this would be just the place to reflect on having wiped out 110,000 lives with atomic bombs. The locals are friendly and welcoming, as though keen to repay the effort in getting there.

After refuelling with an obligatory slice of key lime pie, I hopped onto a trolley bus to get the lie of the land in the fastest time possible. We trundled along leafy streets lined with pastel-painted wooden houses. The homes all had quaint front porches, folded-back shutters, ornate gables and white-picket fences. There

---

[9] The S doesn't stand for anything.

was none of the overt security precautions seen elsewhere in the country. It was peaceful, almost idyllic.

I hopped off at the Southernmost Point Marker, where people were queuing to take 'a selfie' with the concrete buoy. The word selfie makes me shudder. It is a reflection of how far society has fallen that we can no longer ask a stranger to take a picture for fear they will run off with our phone. I also detest how people have to place themselves at the centre of everything and the herd mentality that has gripped social media users. Back in the day, parents use to encourage children to resist peer pressure, with the wise words: 'if they told you to jump off a cliff would you do it?' Now, we have millions of idiots pouring buckets of ice over their heads because it is an online craze.

I eschewed the queue and skilfully stole a photo during a changeover in narcissists. As well as marking the southernmost point of contiguous America, the buoy indicates that Cuba lies only 90 miles away, tantalisingly closer than Miami is to Key West.

I stared wistfully out to sea. Had there been a ferry to Cuba from Miami or Key West, I would have been on it, but now was time for patience.

I headed to Cuba just a few weeks later, arriving in Havana from Spain, where I had marked my 40th birthday alone in a rural farmhouse by gulping down a miniature vodka, neat, in two mouthfuls. I know how to party. Spain was also the departure point for Christopher Columbus, who set out in 1492 to find a westerly sea route to Asia and instead stumbled across the Americas, a continent previously unknown to the Europeans, or a temporarily forgotten continent if you believe the Vikings and the Welsh. Sailing across the ocean blue with a fleet of three vessels, rather than flying with Iberia as I did, Columbus landed first in the Bahamas, then travelled on to Cuba and Hispaniola. Believing he had reached the Indian Ocean, Columbus named the natives he encountered Indians.

Without realising his error, he would make three more westward expeditions in the following decade, reaching the Caribbean islands and Central and South America, and missing out North America entirely. It would be another Italian navigator, Amerigo Vespucci, who would bequeath his name to the continent, after he deduced it wasn't actually part of Asia. But Columbus is recognised as the man who, for better or worse, initiated the European colonisation of the New World and the 'great exchange' of plants, animals and diseases that would transform the continent for ever more.

It being the pre-baggage-allowance era, Columbus took with him on his voyages all the essentials including cats and dogs, chickens, cows, goats, horses, and sheep. Returning home, he, and the traders who followed him, carried exotic treats such as chillies, cocoa, maize, potatoes, tobacco, tomatoes, and possibly even syphilis to enhance life in the Old World.

European diseases proved deadly to the Americas. By the late 1700s, more than two thirds of the indigenous population of North and South America had been wiped out, including the Incas and the Aztecs; the increasing labour shortage leading to the development of the transatlantic slave trade, the repercussions of which still reverberate today.

I must admit that, for most of my life, my knowledge of Native Americans was limited to early school memories of drawing wigwams and totem poles, a favourite Ladybird book telling of Big Chief Sitting Bull's victory over General Custer in the Battle of Little Bighorn, and whatever I gleaned from lusting over cowboys in Western films. Knowing what I do now, I assume they must save the genocide part to teach at university.

The history of the Native American is one of persecution, broken treaties, massacres and, ultimately, attempted extermination. The peaceful co-existence eventually achieved under British rule through the creation of a vast protected reserve between the Appalachian Mountains and the Mississippi River ended as land-hungry Americans raced to settle the entire continent. Beginning with the Indian Removal Act of 1830, they sought to drive the tribes from their ancestral lands into smaller and smaller reservations. The ultimatum was for the Native Americans to give up their nomadic life on the Great Plains or die.

The inevitable wars that followed brought out great savagery on both sides. The Americans settled on a tactic of starving the natives into submission by hunting to near extinction the buffalo herds, which provided their food, shelter and clothing. In the mid-19th century, an estimated 30-60 million buffalo roamed free in the United States. By the end of the century, just 300 remained.

The opening of the transcontinental railway in 1869 accelerated the decimation of the species: hunting parties now crossed the prairies, firing from the windows and roofs of the trains, and leaving behind them a trail of carcasses to rot in the open air. Photographs from the time show immense mounds of bison skulls, providing a permanent record of the scale of the slaughter and the extent of man's inhumanity to animal. It is difficult not to see in them a foreshadowing of the hair and spectacles that one day would be amassed at Auschwitz.

My journey around the US did not provide any glimpses of buffalo or any chance encounters with Native Americans, and the only time I heard mentioned of them was passing by the town of Reno, when an old man remarked that Native Americans love casinos.

His casual comment led me to some interesting facts. There are about 470 casinos in America owned by Indian tribes, including three near that very important city of Yuma. The income from the casinos is used to improve infrastructure in their reservations, to support educational initiatives and to provide social programmes for tribe members. It is a widely believed myth that Native Americans are getting rich on profit distribution from the casinos, but this is rarely the case. Many of the casinos have to service huge debts that paid for their construction, and plenty are struggling to stay afloat.

I would have liked to stay a few days in Key West to drink in its relaxed vibe. Instead, I had to make do with a visit to the Ernest Hemingway house museum, followed by refreshments in his old watering holes.

The American novelist lived in his Key West home from 1931 to 1939. The museum paints him as a disciplined author who wrote from six in the morning until noon, always while standing up as 'writing like travel expands your ass'. Another quote the museum uses to emphasise his strict writing schedule reads: 'My training was never to drink after dinner nor before I wrote nor while I was writing.' It is actually a line taken from *A Moveable Feast* where Hemingway recounts the time he and F Scott Fitzgerald drove a car back to Paris from Lyon - a journey that consumed more alcohol than petrol. Before setting out after breakfast, the pair have a whisky and water; their packed lunch includes a bottle of white wine and Hemingway then buys four more for the afternoon drive. Upon reaching their hotel, they each have three double whiskies, before ordering a carafe of red wine and another bottle of white. With an appetite like that for booze, one would need to start work at six in the morning and finish by noon to ensure sufficient drinking time.

Hemingway's favourite drinking haunt is today festooned with unwashed bras. Ladies, I was told, like to leave behind a memento after visiting the rather grimy Captain Tony's Saloon, which happens to be built around a tree trunk. Dusty bank notes and car number plates are also suspended from the rafters, leaving you inclined to keep a hand over your beer, lest something nasty drops in.

I wasn't tempted to add to the display, nor was I interested in popping into the 'clothing-optional' Garden of Eden bar. I can think of nothing that would put me off a cocktail more than people dancing around in the buff, jangling their bits about.

I departed for Miami with my underclothes intact, and during the four-hour bus ride back, I contemplated the collective cost of the bras abandoned in Key West. It gave new meaning to the notion of disposable income.

NASHVILLE

I KEPT MY PROMISE to myself and flew to Nashville. After so many days spent on trains, the speed of aviation travel impressed me, but I will never feel entirely comfortable hurtling through the sky in an aluminium tube. When you think of it like that, it seems a preposterous form of transport.

In my twenties, I went through a spell of being terrified of flying. It was brought on by a travel companion joking that the engine had cut out as we reached cruising altitude: the imprudent comment left me hypersensitive to changes in engine noise for years and kept me tethered to Europe for my adventures.

What scares me most is the thought of the long drop to earth if something goes wrong. I don't fear train accidents as they are over in a flash, and I rate my chances of just sustaining a few broken limbs. I know that in reality you die pretty sharpish in an air disaster, once the cabin depressurises, but reason has no place up in the sky when you are roller-coaster riding through a bout of severe turbulence.

I conquered my fears by reading a book on the history of aviation. That sounds a greater endeavour than it was, and since I'm not one to mislead, I should clarify it was an illustrated children's book on aviation and the history ended circa 1960. But it made me realise how pathetic I was compared to those pioneering aviators who were willing to risk their lives jumping off cliffs with little more than wooden struts, paper and feathers attached to their backs in the interest of humankind's progression. If it had been left to me, we would still be cowering in the back of caves, grunting and beating each other with clubs. I decided it was time to woman up, and now, whenever a flight gets bumpy, I pretend I am Amelia Earhart crossing the Atlantic Ocean. Unless I've had too much red wine and my cheeks are glowing, then I pretend I am Icarus.

I was over the moon to be going to Nashville. As a child, I was desperately in love with Johnny Cash. Some of my earliest memories involve carefully placing the needle onto a Johnny Cash record and jumping up and down on the sofa playing air guitar with him. Once hormones entered the picture, I would sit transfixed, gazing at his face on an album sleeve and imagining our children. I grew up in a television-free household, so this was quite normal behaviour for a child required to entertain herself.

I loathed his wife June with equal passion, and in the unlikely event of me being called upon in an emergency situation, I would have struggled to bring myself to save her. I thought I was going to burst as I walked through Nashville airport, past the guitars in display cases and the adverts for the new Johnny Cash museum, I was that happy to be in the home of country music. All my life, everyone had derided my taste in music, but now I was allowed to revel in it. Here, I was normal.

I spent half a day in the Johnny Cash museum, devouring every exhibit, before passing the afternoon and evening in an exquisite beery fog, honky tonk hopping along Nashville's neon-lit Broadway, serenaded by cowboys clad in embroidered shirts, rhinestones and fancy boots.

There is a knack to bar hopping in Nashville, and as a novice, I kept mistiming my arrival to coincide with the band changeovers. But I soon worked out the system and also discovered that if I bought a CD and displayed it prominently I was able to shield myself from aggressive demands for tips. Songs such as *Ghost*

Riders and *I Walk the Line* are overplayed to please the tourists, while the local favourites are *Rocky Top*; *If You're Gonna Play in Texas*; and the classic *Save a Horse (Ride a Cowboy)*, which never fails to get the thigh-slapping going.

The national anthem also gets a regular outing in Nashville's honky tonks, always with a dedication to the US Armed Forces. With 20 million veterans in America and 2 million active service personnel and reserves, a cynic might say this is just an easy way to get the tips flowing in, particularly once you factor in all their relatives as well. But there is a sincere respect shown for the military in the United States that extends way beyond the bars. For instance, members of the Armed Forces are thanked for their service and invited to board planes first, along with women and young children. Such reverence is quite extraordinary for a country that has not seen conflict on its home soil since World War II.

These esteemed men and women are the domestic legacy of Washington's interventionist foreign policy in the new world order. There are 7.3 million veterans from the Gulf wars, 6.7 million Vietnam veterans, and 1.5 million who fought in the Korean war during the 1950s.

One statistic which starkly illustrates how the global balance of power has changed is that 95,000 members of the US Armed Forces have died in combat since World War II, while Britain has lost fewer than 7,500 troops.

Of course, the number of enemy combatants and civilians killed in the name of America's vision of freedom is incalculable - estimated to be in the tens of millions - and roundly criticised. The US military has become exactly what Elbridge Gerry, a signatory of the Declaration of Independence, foresaw when he likened a standing (permanent) army to a standing penis: 'An excellent assurance of domestic tranquillity, but a dangerous temptation to foreign adventure.'

It had never entered my mind that the White House's foreign adventures, and misadventures, also left an imprint on American society. In Chicago, I passed a man with a sign that read: 'Help a homeless vet'. I was surprised that highly skilled people such as veterinarians could be left without work. As time passed, I realised my error and I began to notice many a former soldier drifting aimlessly, approaching strangers for money and a sympathetic ear.

It is hard to define Nashville in terms of its aesthetic appeal. I want to describe it as a fairly ugly city, but writing that feels unduly harsh. It has a number of architectural gems from the late 19th century, however, the scale of the modern buildings is so overwhelming that all I retained was an impression of concrete. The river is no thing of beauty either, and the wide roads dwarf what few trees there are.

The city has been booming over the past decade. While the rest of America struggled to emerge from the global financial crisis, job creation and population growth in Nashville have been faster than the national average. A construction drive has seen the government buildings spruced up and a crop of new real estate developments emerge in the downtown area.

Although famously known as Music City, thanks to its 200 recording studios and traffic lights that play country tunes, Nashville's biggest industry is actually healthcare. The healthcare sector contributes nearly $40bn each year to the local economy and provides employment for 250,000 people. By comparison, the entertainment industry is worth $10bn and supports 60,000 jobs. Religious publishing is also big business in Nashville as it sits at the heart of America's bible belt.

But it was the clichéd city, with its holy trinity of live music, beer and good food that I sought, found and fell in love with. The Nashville I encountered was a safe, happy place where everyone is united in a shared love of cowboy music. The hotels even put on free buses to take you to the pub and bring you home at the end of the night.

All country music fans must make a pilgrimage to the Grand Ole Opry once in their lifetime if they are physically and financially able to do so. The Grand Ole Opry is a country music concert that has been broadcast on the radio live from Nashville every weekend since 1925. Still today, the adverts are read out on stage: a deep Tennessee drawl repeatedly interrupts the concert to remind you about the merits of shopping at Boot Barn and Dollar General in case you have forgotten since being told 10 minutes earlier. Given the average age of the audience, though, many most likely will have forgotten.

It is quite a masterful scam selling expensive tickets to people so they can hear sponsored messages read to them, with a little bit of country music thrown in. Nothing ever lives up to its folklore, but maybe I am just bitter because on the night I went the performers played cheesy Christmas tunes country-style. It was an act of barbarism in a beautiful setting.

From Nashville, a reasonably priced day trip will take you to see Memphis and Graceland, the home of Elvis Presley. Elvis versus Johnny Cash is one of the music world's great rivalries, along with the Beatles and the Rolling Stones, Blur and Oasis. At school, the girls who loved Elvis and the Beatles were considered cool, while I, a devoted fan of Johnny Cash, glam rock and George Formby, defied classification. Decades later, their unwarranted supremacy still irked me, so I decided to forego a visit to Graceland; just the thought of being cooped up on a bus with dozens of excitable Elvis fans made me nauseous.

Besides, I had seen more than enough Elvis memorabilia in Nashville's museums. An ostentatious gold-trimmed 1960s Cadillac painted with 40 coats of 'diamond dust pearl' confirmed to me he was a man without taste or virtue, the original Mr Bling. Diamond dust pearl is a mix of crushed diamonds and fish scales, and as a car coating idea that says just one thing to me: drugs.

My intention had been to head off to the bright lights of Las Vegas as the final destination on my American odyssey, but I was so enamoured with the honky tonks that I extended my stay in Nashville instead.

Sometimes the universe gives you a sign that you are correctly fulfilling your destiny and, lo and behold, on my last night in Nashville as I was crowning a stomach full of beer with some delicious wood-smoked meat, rustic baked beans and overcooked vegetables, ZZ Top's *Viva Las Vegas* appeared on the television in front of me.

As I struggled to focus my gaze on the bearded legends, I realised Las Vegas with its show girls and roulette wheels was no place for someone like me, who hates watching other people having fun. I was right where I was meant to be that evening. In that moment of heightened perception, I finally understood I did have impeccable music taste: it was everyone else who was misguided. And I concluded that if I ever wanted to give into alcoholism, Nashville would be the place to do it.

I like to think I would have stayed at Nashville's Union Station Hotel, if I had done some research and known it existed, regardless of its eyewatering room rates. Dating from 1900, the former station is an imposing limestone structure, topped with a clock tower worthy of any church. In its heyday, the station served eight national rail routes as well as the local streetcars. But as the popularity of train travel waned throughout the 1960s and 70s, the building fell into disrepair and after the last train left on 8 October 1979, it was abandoned altogether.

Its potential was fortunately recognised and in 1986, the station began a new life as a luxury hotel. Two $10bn-plus refurbishments have bequeathed a jaw-dropping lobby, restoring the vast barrel-vaulted ceiling, intricate wood carvings and stained-glass windows. It is a fitting use for a former station: travellers once again hurry across the marble floors, dragging their suitcases behind them.

The wooden benches have made way for sofas, and the ticket office sells cocktails and coffees in place of adventures, but the black and white arrivals and departures board still pulls your eye magnetically towards it. As a last-minute discovery, it felt appropriate that I just nipped in for a wee and a wander around, as one would have done back when it was a station, before setting off towards my journey's end in New York.

THE JOURNEY'S END

MY JOURNEY ENDED where it had begun seven weeks earlier, in New York. I had survived without being shot, mugged or any of the other horrors the internet had promised would befall me. It was just days before Christmas and the city was heaving with last-minute shoppers and tourists.

As I ambled about, recoiling at the oily water and rubbish collecting in the gutters, the contrast between New Yorkers and the Americans I had encountered in the west and south of the country was unmistakable. Here, everyone was in a hurry, going about their business with no interest in the people around them, beyond the need to elbow past them. I decided their coldness reflected the climate of the east and determined not to allow this to cloud my newly acquired positive perceptions of Americans.

For the most part, I had found the American people to be friendly and welcoming, keen to impress their country upon me. Admittedly, I encountered only a small slither of society, but those I met were good humoured, generous and courteous - not everyone was out for a tip.

Despite the high crime statistics, Americans don't walk around in fear, but this could be because they always carry a gun or a scalding hot Starbucks coffee, and they mostly drive everywhere.

Americans talk to anyone and have a live-for-today attitude, which means they just get on and do whatever it is they want to do. While this probably stems from the knowledge that life can be snuffed out any second by a well-armed neighbour, colleague or relative, I have to concede they make us Brits seem repressed, not just reserved.

We do have the upper hand when it comes to table manners, though. Americans have not yet mastered knife and fork skills, largely because they consume most of their food with their fingers. It is exhausting to watch the number of times their forks change hand during a meal, but observing this charade is a good distraction from the open-mouthed chewing and talking-while-eating they all seem to delight in. Just as remarkable is the amount of detritus the average American generates while consuming food, beginning with a thousand half-empty sachets of tomato ketchup, mayonnaise and mustard, and ending with mountains of used napkins. (More reasons not to sign up to international climate change protocols.)

Any self-respecting Brit writing on America and its people is obliged to touch upon their misuse and abuse of the English language, but with so much to enrage a pedant, where does one begin?

Well first, one should recognise that after independence there was a campaign to develop a distinct American language in order to assert cultural autonomy from Britain. At the time, British English was being modernised and standardised following the 1755 publication of Samuel Johnson's *A Dictionary of the English Language*. The United States decided to stick with the Early Modern English brought over by the 17th century settlers, and introduced some of their own spelling reforms instead. This helps to explain the preservation until today of archaic terms such as oftentimes and why Americans will take every opportunity to tell you they speak the purest form of English.

Unfortunately, it is true that many of the words we consider to be ugly Americanisms, such as honor, gotten, center and trash, can be found in Shakespeare and other ancient works of English literature.

Another point to remember is that as a nation built on immigration, effective communication would have been more important than grammatical accuracy, and this has allowed for looser syntax and the simplification of language over time. Thus, there is no use explaining to an American that the verbs detrain, deplane and deboard are abominations, when their meaning is clearer than disembark. Or that normalcy is anything but normality, and maths said without the 's' and Lego said with the 's' makes me want to slap them. While their gross misuse of prepositions offends my English ears, I begrudgingly admit it does not affect the meaning of what is being communicated.

Instead, we must focus our attention on fighting back against the Americanisation - or rather the Americanization - of British English, while there is still hope for salvation. America's cultural imperialism means that generations of our children are growing up thinking that petrol stations sell gas, that sidewalk is an acceptable synonym for pavement, and bad can be used as a noun preceded by a possessive. Kids today are more likely to beg for a movie and candy, than a film and sweets. They think regular and grande are actual units for measuring liquids, and instead of biscuits, they want to dunk cookies in their tea and coffee.

If we continue down this route - pronounced 'root' not 'rowt' - it won't be long before pie is being used as a synonym for pizza, leading to mayhem in the north of England, and our neighbours across the Channel start scoffing at us for incorrectly calling main courses entrées, which, if you consult any French person, means starter. Black Friday is now a thing in the UK, Christmas begins in November because of Thanksgiving, the school prom has replaced the end of year disco and out of nowhere, in 2015, we began naming our storms. Series have become seasons, murders homicides and takeaways takeouts. I once even heard a British teenager refer to the police as 'the feds' in an angry rant on the news - so much anger against something that does not exist in our country!

The way I see it, following this brief and superficial study, the Americanisation of our language and culture is the last frontier as the US' seeks the full subjugation of its former colonial master. The War of 1812 didn't end in stalemate in 1815, it is ongoing. Rather than bombs and drones, Washington is using soft power tactics to occupy British hearts and minds.

The infiltration of American slang into the English language accelerated after World War I, with the arrival of the Jazz Age and Hollywood's transition from silent films to 'talkies'. Today, the agents of influence are the Netflix series streaming into homes the length and breadth of the UK. America has stolen our youth away from the BBC - tasked with conditioning them into loyal British subjects - by tempting them with interminable crime dramas, paedophile documentaries and exotic tales of tigers in captivity.

Our English inflections are under siege. Americans will tell you how much they love our accents, but they are set on wiping them out. Why else would they remake *The Office* and *Cracker*? Within a generation, it will be no surprise to hear British people speaking of 'Hairy Potter', 'Down Town Abbey' and 'sqwirls'. I worry for the 'h' on our herbs.

In its most daring attack on our sovereignty, Washington penetrated right to the heart of Britishness, stationing Meghan Markle in the UK to weaken our resistance with hugs instead of handshakes, before stealing away our most handsome prince.

There can be no denying that we are living in the age of matriphagy: when the child eats its mother. Which is why it really upsets me that all this trip has done is make me want to go back and explore the rest of America.

The America that I return to will be different, reshaped following four years of Trump's presidency, the global pandemic and the Black Lives Matters protest movement; a country soon to be eclipsed by China as the world's largest economy. For the history of the United States is still being written.

POSTSCRIPT

I FORGET how many Union stations I passed through while travelling around America, but I remember making the romantic assumption that they honoured the vanquishing side in the Civil War. Only later did I learn it was the functional name given to stations jointly owned by more than one train operator.

Until 1971, intercity passengers in the US were served by dozens of privately owned railway companies. Although their strategic focus was on freight transportation, the firms were legally obliged to provide passenger services as well, in return for being granted land for their rail networks. The first Union station opened in Indianapolis in 1853, when four railroad companies teamed up to provide passengers with a more convenient central facility in place of their individual terminals. (The station is now a Crowne Plaza Hotel, complete with 13 Pullman carriages converted into guest rooms.)

After flourishing in the 19th and early 20th centuries, competition from car ownership and bus and air travel caused a rapid decline in the use of the longer distance passenger services from the 1960s; much freight business was also lost to trucks following the construction of America's interstate highways, forcing several private railroads into bankruptcy.

This prompted Congress to pass the Rail Passenger Service Act of 1970, which led to the formation a year later of Amtrak - the National Railroad Passenger Corporation - to take over intercity passenger services from the ailing private railroads. Of the 26 rail companies in existence at the time, just six said they wished to continue transporting passengers and within years, they too gave up their obligations.

Amtrak inherited untold problems, from dilapidated rolling stock and station facilities to inefficient schedules and routes, and nearly 50 years later, it is still not able to stand on its own feet financially.

In 2019, Amtrak made $3.5bn in revenue, while its capital and operating expenses totalled $4.9bn, leaving the federal government to plug the gap. For a country that spends more than $800bn a year on defence and security, you might think a subsidy of $1.5bn is nothing when balanced against the connectivity the rail network provides.

Amtrak serves more than 500 destinations in 46 states and three Canadian provinces through a network comprising more than 21,300 miles of track, 72 per cent of which is still owned by freight companies[10]. Yet the future of America's great railways has been in doubt in recent years.

In each of his federal budgets, Trump proposed halving Amtrak's funding and terminating all financial support for its 15 long-distance rail routes, which collectively incur an annual operating loss of about $500m. The White House proposal (which Congress repeatedly rejected) would have destroyed the national rail network, removing train services from 23 states and more than 220 towns and cities.

The *Texas Eagle*, one of the long-distance lines under threat, connects 42 cities across seven states. Most passengers do not travel the full 2,728 miles between Los Angeles and Chicago, but

---

[10] This is the chief cause of the delays that blight Amtrak's services as the private freight companies often prioritise their own slow-moving engines ahead of passenger trains.

typically take journeys of less than 300 miles between communities that are many hours' drive from the nearest city or airport. The railway provides essential and affordable services for hundreds of isolated, rural communities, and it is conceivable that the termination of passenger services would lead to the economic decline and even the disappearance of certain towns, in the same way that the arrival of train travel catalysed their growth.

Rather than a drain on federal resources, America's passenger rail network should be considered an economic asset and a treasured part of the country's heritage, alongside the national parks. It was, after all, the transcontinental railways that accelerated the western migration of settlers and helped America become the country it is today. It was also the railways that introduced the first standardised time zones in the US in 1883, and supported America in World War II by facilitating massive troop movements.

Happily, America's 46th president, Joe Biden is a big fan of the railways. One of his 2020 campaign pledges was to deliver a 'second great railroad revolution' as part of his greenhouse gas reduction programme. This would see passenger services throughout the country upgraded with high-speed connections to provide a sustainable alternative to road and aviation, ensuring America's railways are fit for the 21st century and equal in safety to those in Europe and China. For this fantastic proposal to succeed, though, the American people literally need to get on board.

Time and again on my travels around the US, I was struck by how many folk said they had never taken a train. In Europe, it is a rite of passage for school leavers to go interrailing around the continent, and retirees do the same, but in greater luxury. Where are the foreign tourists, the young backpackers and the silver riders trying to tick off all the US states by train? They are missing out on a magical experience in which the journey is as much part of the holiday. By the end, I'll admit you won't want to see another Amtrak sandwich, but the environment will thank you for ditching the car and the plane.

'Nor is it given to any man to know whether, when evening comes, he will need boots for his body or slippers for his corpse.'

Leo Tolstoy, *What Men Live By*

If you enjoyed reading this book, please leave a glowing review on Amazon as I need all the help I can get to bring attention to my work! Thank you!

To view photographs from my rail journey around America and to stay informed about future book launches, follow me on Instagram @thebainsreport. For my comedy work, please follow @lizaarrd